FINDING YOUR
HIDDEN
TREASURE

The Way of Silent Prayer

STILLNESS - VIGILANCE

BENIGNUS O'ROURKE OSA

Liguori

LIGUORI, MISSOURI

Imprimi Potest: Harry Grile, CSsR
Provincial, Denver Province, The Redemptorists

This edition published in 2011 by Liguori Publications,
Liguori, Missouri 63057 USA

To order, call 800-325-9521 or visit www.liguori.org

Published by Darton, Longman and Todd LTD, London, UK
Copyright © 2011

ISBN 978-0-7648-2000-7

Excerpt from 'Emerging' by R. S. Thomas from *R. S. Thomas Collected Poems, 1945 –
1990,* published by Phoenix Press, an imprint of Orion Books (2001).

Excerpt from *The Glass Bead Game* by Hermann Hesse, published by Vintage Classics,
of Random House Group Ltd. (1969).

First published in 2010 by
Darton, Longman and Todd Ltd
1 Spencer Court, 140–142 Wandsworth High Street
London SW18 4JJ United Kingdom

Liguori Publications, a nonprofit corporation, is an apostolate of the Redemptorists.
To learn more about the Redemptorists, visit redemptorists.com.

14 13 12 11 / 5 4 3 2

'God speaks to us in the great silence of the heart.'

Augustine of Hippo

CONTENTS

FOREWORD

Benignus O'Rourke has both rediscovered and modernised the lost art of the monastic chapter as a literary form.

His concentrated and economic prose communicates depth without wasting a word.

Most chapters in *Finding Your Hidden Treasure* are just over a page in length. They are arranged thematically. Each addresses a crucial threshold along the spiritual path.

If you are looking for a book that is eloquent in its simplicity, perceptive in the issues addressed, and will bring comfort in the presence of a God closer to us than we are to ourselves, *Finding Your Hidden Treasure* is a sure-footed guide.

Those of us drawn to silent prayer will feel very much in debt to Benignus O'Rourke for producing this fine volume.

Martin Laird, author of *Into the Silent Land*

INTRODUCTION

A Boyhood Dream

At the age of 16, I made a chance visit to a Cistercian monastery. On the way home from boarding school for the Christmas holidays my friend Joe was breaking the long train journey to visit his brother, who was then a novice at Mount Melleray Abbey in County Waterford. Con and I decided to go with him.

The modern abbey, white stone against the brown-grey Knockmealdown mountains, was startling in its new beauty. And in the 24 hours we spent there I caught a glimpse of a life of prayer, silence and stillness. White-cowled monks moving soundlessly over the shining floors, the quiet, gentle chant that seemed to reflect the holiness of God, the bells sounding in the high tower, everything enclosed in a deep stillness.

All of this cast its powerful spell on my young imagination. Looking back, I realise now that in my earlier days I had already met what I would later come to know as stillness. I had sensed it in my grandmother, Mary Roche. Her home and her life reflected a deep stillness which seemed to flow into my life. As John Banville writes: 'So much of life was stillness then, when we were young, or so it seems now; a biding stillness, a vigilance.'

A few months after my visit to Mount Melleray I asked the priest who was guiding me in discerning my vocation if the life of a contemplative would be right for me. Quietly, he dismissed my dream as fanciful. Without hesitation he said, 'You can take it from me that you have no vocation to the contemplative life.'

I took it from him and, two years later, joined the Augustinian Order for a life based on prayer and active ministry in the world. The longing for the life of Melleray faded, but never completely. That longing was to be fulfilled many years afterwards in a way I could never have predicted. I discovered the prayer of stillness and silence, and its place in Augustine's spirituality. It changed my life and my work. And it is a gift of God that links me with that boyhood dream.

For many years I have tried to share with others the gift of silence and stillness. This book is an attempt to share that gift more widely, and to thank God for it.

Martin Nolan, a fellow Augustinian who has spent about 40 years giving retreats all over the world, says that what people need most to help them on their spiritual journeys is simple. 'First, there is a great hunger for prayer everywhere, which is not being met. Second, people of all ages are asking how best to pray.'

Alan Watts, an Anglican priest who became a Buddhist, was aware of this need when he wrote in *Behold the Spirit* of the 'thousands of souls, in church and out of church, who realize that what they want from religion is not a collection of doctrinal and ritual symbols, nor a series of moral precepts. They want God himself, by whatever name he may be called; they want to be filled with his creative power and life; they want some conscious experience of being at one with Reality itself.'

There is of course no one way of praying, although many of us may have been taught only one way to pray. And there is no 'best' way to pray. Different people pray in different ways, and each of us will pray in different ways at different times.

But there are two golden rules about prayer. One is that we have to pray as we can in the way best suited to us, not in the way we think we ought. So there is no need to change the way we pray if we are happy with it. And the other rule is: the less we pray, the harder it gets. *The more the easier*

So my book is written for the very many people, young and old, in or out of church, who may be struggling in their own attempts to come closer to God and are finding that familiar ways of prayer are not helping, not working.

The more ... the more .
A chi più ha più sarà dato —

PART ONE
OUR LOST TREASURE

1

Sitting There All Peaceful and Quiet

Some time ago an elderly lady complained to me that she could no longer pray. 'Father,' she said, 'I can't pray like I used to. I come here to church after my shopping and sit here all peaceful and quiet. But,' she sighed, 'I can't pray like I used to.'

I tried to suggest that perhaps sitting there all peaceful and quiet *was* prayer. Maybe it was a gift God was offering her at this stage of her life. But she was not convinced. Prayer for her meant keeping her mind on the words, battling with distractions, concentrating. Sitting there all peaceful and quiet would have seemed to her like laziness and failure.

What my parishioner was discovering, in fact, was one of God's loveliest gifts, the purest form of prayer. She rejected it because it was not what she had been taught. And she is not alone. Many people who come to the retreat house where I live, to attend Sunday or daily Mass, or in search of peace and quiet or guidance, share her anxiety about praying.

Many of us will remember being taught that prayer is a lifting of our minds and hearts to God. This teaching can lay a heavy burden on us. We feel that we must make an effort to speak to God, to praise him, to give thanks, to ask for help. We normally use words, thoughts and images, and feel we have to keep our minds fixed on what we are saying.

But there are times when we cannot find the words, or when the well-known prayers which usually inspire and comfort us strike no chord in our hearts. Or we may be singing God's praises while our hearts are heavy, or empty. And our hearts become heavier because our feelings do not match the words.

We are perhaps tired of words, anyway. Tired of asking God in words that have no life in them. Tired of thinking about God. Tired of being talked to about God. Tired of saying prayers that may be beautiful in themselves but are not bringing God closer to us.

Then, perhaps it is best to simplify our prayers and follow the age-old advice, to go from many words to few words, from few words to one word, and from one word into silence. Sometimes when we pray, our words, any words, can be barriers. They come between us and God. The deepest communion with God comes through silence.

There is a form of prayer where we do nothing, where we sit in stillness and silence, not straining or striving. We abandon all words and reflection and we rest. We put ourselves in God's hands and wait in silence, to let God's Spirit pray in us. Sitting there all peaceful and quiet, like the elderly lady in church, is what this kind of prayer is all about.

2

Spiritual Gold

Prayer without words is not new. It is older than Christianity itself and was a rich part of the Christian tradition up to medieval times. It is only in our own lifetime that we have woken up to the fact that here in the West for 600 or so years the treasure of pure, silent prayer has been almost completely forgotten and abandoned, even in religious communities.

The Benedictine monk John Main was one of the first people to make us aware of our loss. Working for the Colonial Service in India, he had discovered the Eastern form of silent meditation and brought it back to Europe and America.

At about the same time young people in their thousands were taking themselves off to the East in search of deeper religious experience. And that caught the public imagination. They learned how to sit still until their minds became quiet, and they discovered a new way of seeing. They were seeing with the eye of the heart, which put them in touch with their deeper selves.

Returning home, some began to explore their own traditions for similar teaching. And in the Christian West they had not far to look. They discovered that much of what they found in Eastern religions was also to be found in Christianity, but no one had told them. Here was a wealth of learning about the power of stillness and silence to lead us to the depths of our own being, where we find God.

Alan Watts, who wrote many wonderful books about Buddhism, said that most of what he found in the East he could have found in the West if only someone had pointed him in the right direction. 'Until I had studied the religions of the East for some years,' he wrote, 'the teaching of Christ and the symbols of Christianity had no real meaning for me. But I do not mean to suggest that a study of Oriental faiths is essential for an understanding of Christianity.' His understanding, he believed, would have been much the same had he read people like Eckhart or Augustine of Hippo.

The kind of spirituality he embraced in the East was available in the great mystics of the West but it had not been made available to ordinary people, he said. 'They do not and cannot be expected to know that the Church has in its possession under lock and key, or maybe the sheer weight of persons sitting on the lid, the purest gold of mystical religion.'

Many others have echoed what Alan Watts said. The Jesuit William Johnson, whose books have helped to bridge the gap between Eastern and Western religions, met opposition from some readers who asked, 'Why go to the East? It is all in Augustine.' And the monk Thomas Merton believes it was his own 'Augustinian bent' that made him receptive to the spiritual wisdom of the East.

It was views such as these that set me looking for what Augustine had to say about finding God in silence and I have been on a treasure hunt ever since. This book is a result of that search.

3

We Shall Find God

It has been a great joy for me, translating Augustine over the years and finding words that do justice to the music of his Latin. There is a wealth of spiritual gold hidden among the five million or more words that he wrote. Hidden, because we come across it unexpectedly in his books, letters and sermons and in his commentaries on sacred scripture. Sometimes it is just a few nuggets, buried within a chapter.

Augustine had discovered for himself, as no one in the West had before him, the mystery of God who hides himself within us. And he realised that silence reveals God to us as nothing else can. If we journey in stillness to the centre of our being, he tells us, we shall find our true selves and we shall find God who, to use Augustine's own words, 'is nearer to us than we are to ourselves'.

Augustine constantly calls us to return to our hearts and it is about this journey inward that I want to write. He has not written a book about the journey, though he wrote countless books. But if we sift through his writing and piece together the fragments of his thinking, he offers us a clear path to help us find our way to God, who is within.

At the time I discovered silent prayer, or the prayer of the heart as it is sometimes known, I was struggling with the round of prayer which was very much part of our lives as a community of priests. As head of a boys' boarding school and of a large religious community I felt that the prescribed daily prayers were not giving me the strength to cope.

So I started to get up an hour earlier than I used to. Sitting quietly in a peaceful room looking out on the priory garden brought a peace that helped me face the day. In the evening, a quiet time in the school chapel helped dissolve the built-up emotions of the day and restored some sanity.

One evening, as I came out of chapel and greeted a group of the boarders heading for their dormitories, I heard one in a loud whisper say, 'What's got into old Ben tonight? He's in a good mood!'

What I suspect had been happening in that time of silence in the chapel was that I had shed the day's weariness and a kind of spontaneity had been recovered. After being an Augustinian friar for 27 years I realised that what was missing in my prayer was silence. A little late in the day I had at last started on the inward journey to my own heart.

John Chapman, who was Abbot of Downside in the 1930s, lamented that he had spent so many years knowing nothing about praying in silence. 'I could have been in it, with immense profit, 22 years ago or more,' he wrote in his letters, 'but no one told me it was possible.'

I too regret that it took me so many years to find the gold of silent prayer. In the chapters that follow I shall try to share what, with the help of many teachers, I have since found at the heart of silence.

4

Return to Your Heart

For those who may not know much about him, Augustine of Hippo grew up in North Africa, in the remote part of the Roman Empire that is now Algeria. His mother Monica was a Christian. His father, Patricius, was a pagan.

Augustine had a restless and troubled youth and from his late teens spent many fruitless years searching outside himself for truth, happiness and fulfilment. When he was about 33, after much mental torment and uncertainty, he made the life-changing discovery that what he was seeking was within himself.

All we need to guide us, he realised, is to be found in our own hearts. There, in the depths of our being, are truth and goodness and love. And these are to be found there because the source of all life is within, the God who has made his home in us.

Augustine records this breakthrough in his *Confessions.* 'You were there before my eyes,' he proclaims, 'but I had deserted even my own self, and I did not find the God of my own heart' (*Confessions* 5.2).

And so we get the great lament: the lament that Augustine had taken so long to discover that God had made his home in him; that he had spent half a lifetime searching in the wrong places for what he needed most. And all the time he had been seeking God, God had never been absent. This is what he wrote:

> Late have I loved you, beauty ever old yet ever new! Late have I
> loved you!
> You were within me, but I was outside.
> There I sought you, as I rushed about among the beautiful things
> you had made.
> You were with me, but I was not with you.
> The beautiful things of this world kept me far from you.
> You called. You cried.
> You burst through my deafness. You scattered my blindness.
> I breathed your fragrance, and now I pine for you.
> I tasted you, and I hunger and thirst for you.
> You touched me, and I burn with desire for your peace.

From the moment Augustine realised that God was not outside, one of the great adventures of life for him became the journey inwards. His discovery led him to accepting Christ and his gospel and for the rest of his life he loved God passionately. He ceaselessly urged all those to whom he later preached or wrote to return to their hearts and seek God within. Only there, he told them, would they find rest and peace for their unquiet souls.

'Come back to your heart,' he implored. 'In your inner self Christ has made his home. In your inner self you will be renewed in God's image. And in his image you will recognise your creator.'

For Augustine, returning to our heart is the key to discovering who we are and to discovering God.

5

Searching for Truth and Wisdom

As Brian Lowery, founder of the Augustinian community in San Gimignano, said during a retreat, 'Augustine is probably more popularly known for what he was converted from than what he was eventually converted to. His earlier life with its youthful sexual wanderings and brash arrogance is more fascinating to most people than his later life as a monk, mystic and bishop. Someone once said he was a saint that had his cake and ate it too.'

When he was born, in Thagaste in 354, Augustine's mother did not have him baptised. Instead, she made the sign of the cross on his forehead to claim him for Christ. As a young boy he was a believer of sorts, and as a young man, however much he poured scorn on her religion, he would always keep respect for the name of Jesus.

When Augustine writes his life story, in his *Confessions*, we read of a soul's struggles to be itself. We see how his inner life, at every step, was linked with his very deep need of God. But time and again he resisted taking the road that would lead him there because, as he said, he was 'led astray by the mists of a befouled heart'.

Augustine had a wayward adolescence. Success in his career went side by side with deep unhappiness. The conflict between his sensual life and his search for truth and wisdom and for God made him sick at heart.

A gifted scholar who had won major prizes in public speaking, he studied law and philosophy before opting for a career in teaching, first in his home town and then in Carthage and Rome, where he became known as a very special teacher. On the eve of his thirtieth birthday he moved to Milan – the centre of the Empire – to become professor of rhetoric and the city's public orator, and to seek honour and wealth.

At this point, Augustine says, his spiritual life was at its bleakest. It was then that he came under the influence of the great Bishop Ambrose. This was a turning point in his life and prepared the way for him to follow Christ.

His moment of conversion took place in a garden near Milan, in August 386. Almost his first instinct, Augustine tells us, was to find time 'to be still and see God'. He resigned his post as professor of rhetoric and, with a group of close friends including his mother Monica and his son Adeodatus, withdrew to a villa in the country. In the foothills of the Alps they set up a little community, lived a life of friendship, prayer and discussion, and worked on the grape harvest. The following spring, they returned to Milan to enrol and prepare for baptism.

At the Easter Vigil on the night of 24–25 April 387 Augustine, his friend Alypius and his son were baptised by Bishop Ambrose. Augustine left Italy for his homeland soon afterwards, hoping to find a place where he and his little group might be most useful in God's service. There, in the city of Hippo, he agreed reluctantly to be ordained as a priest at the insistence of the Christian community and, soon afterwards, as bishop.

Augustine worked and travelled tirelessly over the next 40 years and became one of the great leaders of the Christian church as preacher, writer, monk and bishop. The greatest philosopher in his day since Aristotle, he became one of Christianity's most influential theologians. Augustinian thought is a common strand in both Catholicism and Protestantism today.

Although he always loved the life of solitude, Augustine believed that the search for God was best pursued in the company of friends. He lived in community even as a bishop, whenever his travels allowed.

In community he prayed the prayer of the Church but he was conscious, too, of the importance of prayer without words. 'Prayer at its deepest is more than words.'

6

God Dwells Within

Augustine always sees the spiritual journey not as a going out, to find God outside, but as a journey inwards. 'He bade me shut the door of our secret chamber and pray in secret,' he writes. 'That is, in the soundless secret places of our hearts. For we pray to him in the silence of our hearts.'

The basis of true prayer for Augustine is the promise Jesus gave that he would live in us when he said to his disciples, 'Make your home in me as I make mine in you.' And after his last meal with his disciples Jesus told them: 'I shall not leave you orphans. I shall come to you. In a short time the world will no longer see me; but you will see that I live and you also will live. On that day you will know that I am in my Father and you in me and I in you' (John 14:18–20).

A little later, Jesus said: 'Anyone who loves me will keep my word, and my Father will love him, and we shall come to him and make our home in him' (John 14:23).

Which is why Augustine urges us: 'Wheresoever you are, wheresoever you may be praying, he who hears you is within you, hidden within. For he who hears you is not merely by your side, and you have no need to go wandering about, no need to be reaching out to God as though you would touch him with your hands.

Wheresoever you are, wheresoever you may be praying, he who hears you is within you, hidden within.'

Several centuries later Meister Eckhart, one of the great mystics, taught: 'You need not seek him here or there, he is no further than the door of your heart; there he stands patiently awaiting whoever is ready to open up and let him in. No need to call to him from afar: he can hardly wait for you to open up. He longs for you a thousand times more than you long for him.'

In his poem 'Emerging' R. S. Thomas, a Welsh clergyman, explores the true nature of prayer.

> I would have knelt
> long, wrestling with you, wearing
> you down. Hear my prayer, Lord, hear
> my prayer. As though you were deaf, myriads
> of mortals have kept up their shrill
> cry, explaining your silence by
> their infirmness.
> It begins to appear
> this is not what prayer is about.
> It is the annihilation of difference,
> the consciousness of myself in you,
> and you in me.

7

Looking in the Right Place

There is a story told by the American-born teacher, Gangaji, in *The Diamond in your Pocket*, of a thief who stole only the most exquisite gems. He would hang around the diamond district to see who was buying the gems, so that later he could pick their pockets.

One day the thief saw a well-known diamond merchant buy the jewel he had been waiting for all his life. It was the most pristine, the purest of diamonds. Very excited, the thief followed the diamond merchant as he boarded the train, getting into the same compartment. He spent the entire three-day journey trying to pick the merchant's pocket and steal the diamond.

When the diamond merchant got off the train the pickpocket followed. Finally, very frustrated, he walked up to the merchant and asked how he had hidden the diamond from him.

'Well, I saw you watching me in the diamond district,' the diamond merchant replied, 'and I suspected you were a pickpocket. So I hid the diamond where I thought you would be least likely to look for it – in your own pocket.' He then reached into the thief's pocket and pulled out the diamond.

It is the same for our own buried treasure.

'Your own hidden treasure,' Gangaji writes, 'is in your pocket right now, in the pocket of your heart.'

Augustine's great discovery that within each one of us, in the depths of our hearts, lies hidden treasure changed his life and it can change ours. 'How much treasure we have within us,' he declares, 'but we do not dig for it!' Most of us, of course, could reply that we do not know, perhaps have never been shown, where or how to start looking for it.

Matthew's Gospel tells us that Jesus in one of his parables likens the kingdom of God to hidden treasure. Jesus said to the crowds: 'The kingdom of heaven is like treasure hidden in a field which someone has found; he hides it again, goes off in his joy, sells everything he owns and buys the field. Again, the kingdom of heaven is like a merchant looking for fine pearls; when he finds one of great value he goes and sells everything he owns and buys it' (Matthew 13:44–46).

If we knew just how much treasure is within us we would surely take time in our busy lives to search for it, to find the pearl of great price buried in the field of our lives. We would make time to spend in God's presence.

If we are prepared to sit in silence and journey to the still centre of our being we shall discover that we have everything within us for our spiritual journey, and there are blessings at each step along the way. What we find on the journey will be different for each one of us. The journey may look the same, but each one's story is unique. We each find our own truth, our own treasure.

As a famous sculptor said of one of his pupils, 'I showed her where to find gold, but the gold she found was truly her own gold.'

8

Knitting Before the Face of God

How we each find our own treasure is illustrated for me by a delightful story in Metropolitan Anthony's *School for Prayer*. He tells about an old lady who visited him shortly after he became a priest in the Orthodox church. She wanted his advice about prayer. For 14 years she had been praying 'the Jesus Prayer' almost continually, she said, and had never experienced God's presence at all.

'If you speak all the time, you don't give God a chance to get a word in,' the priest responded.

'What shall I do?' she asked.

The priest advised her to go to her room after breakfast, put it right, and place her armchair in a strategic position that would leave behind her back all the dark corners into which things are pushed so as not to be seen.

'Light the little lamp before the ikon that you have, and first of all take stock of your room,' he told her. 'Just sit, look round and try to see where you live because I am sure that if you have prayed all these fourteen years it is a long time since you have seen your room. And then take out your knitting and for fifteen minutes knit before the face of God, but I forbid you to say one word of prayer. You just knit, and try to enjoy the peace of your room.'

She didn't think it was very pious advice, Metropolitan Anthony writes, but she took it. Some time later the old lady returned, saying she had done just what he advised. 'It works,' she told him. 'I got up, washed, put my room right, had breakfast, came back, made sure there was nothing that would worry me, and then I settled into my armchair and thought, "Oh how nice, I have fifteen minutes in which I can do nothing without feeling guilty!" And I looked around and for the first time in years I thought, "Goodness, what a nice room I live in."'

Then she said, 'I felt so quiet because the room was so peaceful. There was a clock ticking but it didn't disturb the silence. Its ticking just underlined the fact that everything was so still, and after a while I remembered that I must knit before the face of God, so I began to knit. And I became more and more aware of the silence.

'The needles hit the armrest of my chair, the clock was ticking peacefully, there was nothing to bother about, I had no need of straining myself. Then I perceived that this silence was not simply an absence of noise, but that the silence had substance. It was not an absence of something but a presence of something. The silence had a density, a richness, and it began to pervade me. The silence around began to come and meet the silence in me.

'All of a sudden I perceived that the silence was a presence. At the heart of the silence there was Him who is all stillness, all peace, all poise.'

PART TWO
BE STILL AND KNOW

9

Discovering God in Silence

Waiting for God in silence, being still so that God may reveal his presence, is part of the teaching of the Scriptures.

In Lamentations we read: 'It is good that one should wait quietly for the salvation of the Lord … It is good to sit alone in silence' (Lamentations 3:26–28). And in 1 Kings we find the story of the prophet Elijah who, in a most unexpected way, found God in the silence. Elijah is fleeing for his life. He takes refuge in a cave on Mount Horeb, but is called to stand outside the cave because God is to pass by.

'Then a great and powerful wind tore the mountains apart and shattered the rocks before the Lord, but the Lord was not in the wind. After the wind there was an earthquake, but the Lord was not in the earthquake. After the earthquake came a fire, but the Lord was not in the fire. And after the fire came a gentle whisper.' When Elijah heard it he pulled his cloak over his face and went out and stood at the mouth of the cave, and God spoke to him (1 Kings 19:11–13).

The Psalms sing in many places of discovering God in silence. In Psalm 62 we read 'For God alone my soul waits in silence.' And in the King James version of the Psalms we come across this lovely advice: 'Commune with the Lord upon your bed in silence and be still' (Psalm 4). Best-known of all is the line from Psalm 46, 'Be still and know that I am God.' This is the invitation and the promise to which Augustine constantly returned all his life.

In the New Testament we read that Jesus loved to spend time alone with his Father. Early in the morning he would take himself off to the hills to pray. Sometimes he would spend the whole night in prayer. Luke's Gospel tells us: 'His fame spread more and more, and many people came to listen to him in order that he should heal them of their illnesses. But he often withdrew to lonely places to pray' (Luke 5:16).

And when Jesus comes to visit Lazarus and his two sisters, Martha and Mary, at Bethany we find that the only thing Mary wants to do is to sit at the feet of Jesus and listen to him. When she shows no sign of coming to help Martha with the supper, Martha complains to Jesus. He gently defends her sister. 'Martha, Martha,' Jesus says. 'You are worried and upset about many things, but only one thing is needed. Mary has chosen the better part, and it will not be taken away from her.'

The tradition grew quickly in the early Church that sitting in silence and stillness, that 'better part', led the way to inner peace, the way of experiencing the mystery of God.

We need only remember the Apostle Paul's words in his letter written to the Christian community in Rome shortly after Christ's death: 'The Spirit too comes to help us in our weakness, for, when we do not know how to pray properly, then the Spirit personally makes our petitions for us in groans that cannot be put into words' (Romans 8:26–27).

Paul's words were echoed by Augustine, who tells us: 'When we pray we have no need of spoken word. Sometimes the tongue is silent and the soul is sighing. That means that God is being prayed to inside, in the room of your heart.'

10

Choosing the Better Part

Augustine links the story of Martha and Mary with Psalm 46. Mary, he says, had truly heard the psalm's promise, 'Be still and know that I am God.' He sees the scene this way.

'While Martha was busy seeing to all the serving, Mary was sitting at the Lord's feet, and listening to his words. One was working hard, the other sitting still, doing nothing. One was feeding others, the other was being fed. Martha was absorbed in the matter of how to feed the Lord; Mary was absorbed in the matter of how to be fed by the Lord. Martha was preparing a banquet for the Lord; Mary was already revelling in the banquet of the Lord.'

In medieval times the unnamed author of *The Cloud of Unknowing* pictures Mary gazing on Jesus with all the love of her heart. 'Nothing she saw or heard could budge her, but there she sat, completely still, with deep delight. From "this part" nothing on earth could move her ... She had other work to do that Martha did not understand.'

Sitting still and remaining quiet in the Lord's presence, like Mary, may be hard for some who are just setting out on the journey into silence. Others will find it easier.

A priest serving a rural parish in Ireland tells the story of an old lady who was housebound for many years with arthritis. He had called in, and sat for a while to chat. 'I suppose, Brigid,' he said, 'you have time to say lots of prayers for us all.'

'Indeed, Father,' she answered, 'I must confess that I don't say many prayers. You see it's like this,' she said. 'I begin to say the Our Father and I say "Our Father," and I think how wonderful it is to be able to call him father. And that seems so wonderful that I can't get any further. I just sit and wonder at it.' Without being taught, Brigid had discovered the truest form of prayer.

Now, most of us pray in the way we have been taught. And the way we pray reflects, or perhaps even fashions, our idea of God. If we fear him, our prayer will be anxious. If we know God as a loving father, then our prayer will be more like Brigid's. So if we are not happy with our prayer we may need to look closely at our notion of God.

11

Our Notion of God

Many of us have been brought up to see God as one who *chooses* us, or who *calls* us, a demanding God who selects us for some purpose. We are not sure what his plan for us is. We worry about our response. We worry about becoming indifferent. We worry about thwarting his will for us. But always we feel there is an insistent call: to improve our lives, to change our ways, to be of more service to others.

What torment this can lead to! Some people are scared of coming close to God in case he asks for more, demands more, or demands more than we are prepared to give.

If this is our notion of God we can become discouraged in prayer. We may feel we are failing to pray properly. We blame ourselves. We feel we are not making enough effort, that we are not concentrating, or that our faith is not strong enough. Because we feel that God is calling us to put our best efforts into pleasing him we try to make a greater effort. If we fail again, we lose heart. And then we are in a vicious circle.

The popular idea of a 'choosing' God, the theologian Urs von Balthasar tells us, is at odds with the God he finds in the writings of Augustine. The God he meets there is before all else a God who draws us to himself to give rest to our restless hearts, the one who wishes to bring us into his peace.

Augustine's God is simply the God who comes to us, indeed who has already come, to give rest to our troubled hearts and minds. God of course does choose people, does call people, but this is not where Augustine's relationship with God begins. 'You made us so that we long for you, and our heart is restless until it rests in you,' Augustine writes in his *Confessions* (1.1).

'God is delight,' he declares, 'and we rest in delight with him, called home from the noise that is around us to the joys that are silent. Why do we rush about to the top of heaven and the bottom of earth,' he asks, 'looking for him who is here at home with us, if only we could be at home with him?'

So prayer for Augustine was not an encounter with a choosing or judging or demanding God, a God up there, or out there. Prayer for him, first of all, was an invitation to rest in the God who dwells in our hearts.

Taking Augustine as one of our guides into deeper prayer changes our notion of God and can liberate us from the mistaken feeling that we are failing or not doing enough in our prayer life. It is not our own efforts that will lead us into prayer. We cease from effort and allow God to do all.

Inner game of prayer

12

A Mother's Story

On the day that the mother of three young boys was told she was seriously ill, she sat by the river and wrote the following lines:

The river flows eternally, just as your spirit is flowing through me.
At first just a ripple on the surface of my being, like the touch
  of gentle rain on my skin.
Life continues and the ripple begins to fade, but you are growing
  beneath the surface in the depth of my soul.
There is no great surge of energy or overpowering event, just a
  gradual beautiful feeling of coming home to be with you.

Since that day, there have been many months of treatment both in and out of hospital, and of physical and emotional pain. There have been times when she has felt she has 'been no use to anybody' and worried about 'letting the boys down'.

But when she went for a scan, which was going to take an hour, she took along a tape on the prayer of stillness. 'I enjoyed the tape. It was just peaceful. I didn't pray,' she told me some time later. 'It was amazing. I listened more and more over the next few days and felt at peace with my situation. But why, I wondered, when I am feeling so angry?'

This introduction to the prayer of silent waiting started her on a spiritual journey which 'has been truly life-changing'. And the young mum described some of her journey for me.

She remembers, in early childhood, a feeling of comfort and warmth when at Mass, or thinking about Jesus, and being drawn to attending the service of Benediction with her father. 'I remember vividly the feeling of being special and feeling that everyone was special and cherished,' she wrote in her email.

'But as I grew older, the God and the faith I fell in love with at the age of six grew further and further away. God became a fearful figure who governed and watched everything and would punish us, either in this life or the next, for any misdemeanour. The God I was being taught about became unrecognizable.

'I now believe the Jesus I experienced at the age of six to be the same loving Jesus as Augustine discovered. He offers us love, unconditional love. We can't blame him when life seems hard. What we do with the love we receive from God can protect us not from suffering but from how that suffering affects us and those we love.

'At one stage in my life the idea that Jesus is always with me terrified me, as if he was waiting to catch me out. But now the awareness that Jesus is always with me, not to punish or chastise me but to share in my happiness and sadness like a best friend, brings me nothing but comfort.'

13

Take a Little Word

There are many ways of beginning the inward journey to our own hearts. We shall each find the way that suits us best.

But *The Cloud of Unknowing* suggests one very simple way. 'When you sit down to pray in quietness and feel that God is calling you to this kind of prayer, then simply lift up your heart in a loving way. To the God who created you, the God who rescued you. To the God who is now calling you to this way of being with him in silence.

'This simple reaching out to God is enough,' the fourteenth-century writer assures us. It is prayer in itself. 'If you wish, you can enfold this reaching out to God in a single word,' he says. 'Take a little word, of one syllable. The shorter the better. Maybe a word like "God" or "love". Choose any word you like, a word of one syllable that you like best. Fix this word to your heart, so that whatever happens it will not go away. *GRACE*

'This word is your protection, whether you are at peace or disturbed. With this word you beat on the cloud that stands between you and God. With this word you can beat down any other thoughts that assail you. Any other thoughts that come can be met with this one little word. Good thoughts as well as disturbing ones. Stay with

43

your word, and you will find that all other thoughts will not trouble you for long.'

The tradition of using one simple word or phrase in this way goes back to a contemporary of Augustine's, John Cassian. In the fourth century he wrote this about keeping prayer as simple as possible: 'Take a short line of a psalm and it shall be your shield and buckler.'

Rowan Williams advises that it does not matter at first how much time we give to our silent prayer, so long as we can give some regular time. 'The challenge is to find enough time to become quiet enough and still enough,' he says.

'Somebody once said that the deepest problem in prayer is often not the absence of God but the absence of me. I'm not actually there. My mind is everywhere. So take a few deep breaths, and use a simple formula like the Orthodox "Lord Jesus Christ, Son of God, have mercy."'

Familiar formulae and rhythms that come naturally actually matter, the Archbishop writes: 'I've sometimes advised people to try to find a verse of a hymn that means something to them or just a single phrase. Things that people only half remember but phrases that stick and, if you let them, sit in your mind.

'That's a beginning of being there. And when you are there God can relate to you. God cannot speak to you if you are not actually there.'

14

Coming Home

The journey inward which Augustine invites us to make is a kind of homecoming.

For Augustine, the heart is not the place of emotions but the place of richest, deepest thought and peace. It is the centre of our being, where we are totally ourselves, our deepest selves. In allowing ourselves to wander outside, we lose touch with ourselves.

'Why do you want to drift so far away from yourself?' he asks. 'Turn back from your idle wandering. Return to your Lord, He is waiting. You have become a stranger to yourself. You do not recognise yourself. And you seek for Him who created you!'

If we are a long way from ourselves, he is saying, how can we come near to God? To return is to find our true home, to find our paradise on earth. This is a bold promise. But Augustine's reason for making it is that when we journey inward it is not just our true self that we find. We find God who has made his home within us.

When we return to our hearts we find rest and peace within in that place of solitude where Christ awaits us to welcome us home.

So at the start of our journey we need to call ourselves back from wandering outside ourselves, from always searching outside for happiness and truth. Our opening prayer could be Augustine's

'Come, O Lord, and stir our hearts. Call us back to yourself. Kindle your fire in us and carry us away. Let us scent your fragrance and taste your sweetness. Bid us love you and hasten to your side.'

Then we try to let our thoughts settle. We cease from effort and allow God to take over. It is a long journey, but he will do everything.

This is a form of prayer, Abbot Chapman reminds us, in which God does all while we wait and wonder. 'Consequently give yourself to prayer, when you can, and trust in God that he will lead you, without your choosing your path. Wait for pressure from him. Do not act unless you must. Let him take the initiative ... If you cannot pray in the least, and only waste time, and moon, and wander, still hold on.'

He also tells us: 'It is better to remain with God, apparently doing nothing in particular, than to make the grandest and most elaborate meditations' (Chapman Letters).

ALLOW GOD 2 TAKE OVER.
Let go of everything
hold on to God only.

15

Trying to Do All the Right Things

The first time she was introduced to silent prayer a teacher friend of mine in Stafford had a great sense of coming home to God. 'When I came to pray before, all the tenseness in my life seemed to be accentuated. I had had 40 years in a classroom of difficult children,' she explained, 'and anxiety each evening nursing an elderly relative.

'I was trying to do all the "right" things to reach God and to come into his presence – formal rosaries and litanies, and daily Mass – plus going through stages of adoration, contrition, thanksgiving and supplication. It all depended on *me*, and my efforts and my concentration. I was exhausted, felt isolated and cut off from the Church, resentment possessing me, faith draining away.

'The first time I tried still prayer, after hearing a talk explaining it, I could not believe the relief as that tension began to melt away. Gradually as I moved into stillness and relaxation I forgot all about myself, aware only of God's presence in the sound of the wind in the trees, in the sound of the birds. And traffic noises seemed very far away. The more I tried, the more did I feel a part of God's creation, and that it mattered to God that I was there, in it.

'I have now become increasingly aware of the presence of God in the very centre of my being, sustaining me, giving me life. But it is not just a presence. I am aware of a deeply personal relationship, a very intimate and loving relationship with this great God. It is a very real relationship, such that I couldn't have with anyone else.

'At this moment of prayer, I think it is the only time I am completely honest with God, not trying to be anyone else, to compete with anyone else, not having to hide anything at all from him. I am finding a new freedom from all the things that fastened me down before – resentments, shyness, self-centredness. And above all it is giving me new faith and trust. It brings life and colour to all the other times when I pray, especially during the Liturgy of the Hours and Mass.

'Silent prayer has become a "must" in my life because it seems that God has not only taken over my prayer time for me, but my life as well, healing me of all that has gone before. I feel I have come home to God. All wretchedness seems to dissolve away in his life-giving presence.'

16

A Quiet Place

In our journey into silence we are not left on our own. What we are invited to do is to find a quiet place and set aside some time.

To find a quiet place where we can rest and allow the Lord to gather us into his peace we do not have to look far. That place is in ourselves, but we have never been shown how to find it.

'Leave behind all noise and confusion,' Augustine counsels. 'Look within yourself and see whether there be some sweet hidden place within where you can be free from noise and argument, where you need not be carrying on your disputes, and planning to have your own stubborn way. Hear the word in quietness that you may understand it.'

To reach the quiet oasis of solitude within we first have to try to bring our body, mind and spirit into a state of quietness. But the more we try to bring our mind to inner quiet, the more it seems to rebel. In a little poem of four lines, 'The Balloon of the Mind', W. B. Yeats likens the mind to a balloon that is tossed around by the wind, and imagines his hands bringing it under control:

> Hands, do what you're bid!
> Bring the balloon of the mind

That bellies and drags in the wind
Into its narrow shed.

Fortunately there are techniques that will help us bring the mind into its narrow shed. Attending to posture and to our breathing will help us find the still centre of our being. The general advice can be summed up in a few words: be attentive and open; sit still; sit straight; breathe slowly, deeply and naturally. belly - baby

So, if our back and our body allow it, we learn to sit on an upright chair with spine straight, head erect and chin tucked in. Our hands are on our lap; our feet firmly planted on the ground.

We need to sit alert, relaxed and receptive. We close our eyes or lower them to the ground. Or we might prefer to fix our gaze on one thing – an icon, a light, a flower. We begin by taking a few deep breaths as we start to relax. Then we observe our breathing. We do not force it. We do not do anything except watch our breathing for as long as we can.

We choose our phrase or our word and abandon all effort except to repeat that little word or phrase. We come back to our word, without annoyance or upset, whenever we find we have wandered. Gently, come back to the centre, to where Christ is, in the centre of our heart.

And we keep doing this no matter how many times the mind bobs about in any wind that blows. No matter how often we have to drag the mind back to its narrow shed, we do not get bothered or give up. We rest and leave everything in God's hands.

17

Wait for the Lord

We may sometimes become aware that the wonderful invitation to enter into the quiet place within is in conflict with our present state of mind or feelings. We hear the invitation but our mood is contrary. What are we to do?

I remember that once, on a long journey in Ireland with the train running late, I found myself at an unscheduled stop at Kildare. Looking through the misty window I found myself staring at a poster on the station billboard. It was advertising holidays in Ireland. The picture was one of utter peace. It showed a cloudless blue sky, a still lake, with not a ripple on the smooth water, and blue-grey mountains behind. Standing beside the peaceful lake was a man in a deerstalker hat, a fishing rod in his hand, a little dog at his side, and a hamper a few yards away. The caption read, 'Tranquillity'.

At that moment, with my view from the carriage window one of grey, louring skies, a steady drizzle, a drab railway station, and a weary feeling of having been already five hours on the train, I found the scene of tranquillity on the poster almost mocking.

When we settle down to our prayer of silence, sometimes the promise of peace and tranquillity may also seem a mockery. Our mood may be one of anxiousness or dogged resistance, or we may be full of anger, or depressed. We try to be true to our prayer word, but there is no easing of the mood we are in.

This is the time to be prepared to wait, to sit still and wait long enough for the clouds of weariness, or rebellion, or worry to lift and our thoughts and feelings to become quiet. In the words of a modern contemplative, 'You must wait in silence from day to day, sometimes from hour to hour. And then the things that are meant to happen will happen. Sometimes there will be straws in the wind, sometimes not even that; you may just have to allow yourself to be carried along by the current.'

So even if it takes longer than we expect, we wait. Augustine encourages us: 'Wait for the Lord. Be firm. Let your heart take courage and wait for the Lord.'

Meister Eckhart, in one of his sermons, likens the person coming into prayer to a damp log that is placed on the fire. It takes time for the log to be warmed and catch fire. 'In order that the wood may catch fire and be penetrated completely time is needed, because the wood and the fire are so dissimilar. At first the fire warms the wood and makes it hot. Then the wood starts smoking and spitting and crackling, because the two are so dissimilar. But as the wood gets hotter it gets quieter. The more the wood gives up to the fire, the more peaceful it is, until at last it really turns to fire' (Sermon 12).

Sometimes it is in our darkest moments, if we are able to wait, that we catch fire.

Let me catch fire -

18

The Din in the Mind

Discovering inner peace is not always easy, as Augustine himself found. In his *Confessions* he recalls: 'The sound of your secret melody I could not catch no matter how hard I tried. My heart was deafened by the din of my mind.'

Augustine would interpret the third commandment, to keep the Sabbath day holy, as an invitation to the stillness of mind and heart we are seeking. 'The Third Commandment calls us to quietness of heart, tranquillity of mind,' he preached in one of his sermons. 'This is holiness. Because here is the Spirit of God. This is what a true holiday means, quietness and rest.'

And he went on: 'Unquiet people recoil from the Holy Spirit. They love quarrelling. They love argument. In their restlessness they do not allow the quiet of the Lord's Sabbath to enter their lives.

'Against such restlessness we are offered a kind of Sabbath of the heart. As if God were saying, "Stop being so restless. Quieten the uproar in your minds. Let go of the idle fantasies that fly around within." God is saying, "Be still and see that I am God."

'But you, so restless, refuse to be still. You are like the Egyptians tormented by gnats. These, the tiniest of flies, always restless, flying about aimlessly, swarm at your eyes, giving no rest. They are back as

53

soon as you drive them off. Just like the futile fantasies that swarm in our minds. Keep the commandment,' he says. 'Beware of the plague.'

When we rest in stillness and try to quieten the uproar in our minds, at first our heads may seem more full of noise than before we started. We become aware of the gnats that plague us. This is because we are now more conscious of what we are thinking.

Some people will become discouraged if, after waiting ten or 15 minutes, nothing seems to happen and the mind is still racing. But if we are patient and are prepared to stay in the silence our thoughts begin eventually to quieten. Instead of a dozen thoughts a minute we may find ourselves dwelling on just one thought.

If we feel we are making little progress on our journey into silence we try not to worry, and we try not to become intense. Abbot Chapman gives us good advice: 'Intensity in prayer causes fatigue. It doesn't do any good to the prayer. It is better to be quite peaceful, without effort, except the effort to remain at peace.'

On a visit to the United States an English archbishop was being interviewed by an eager young woman reporter. She put some searching questions. She asked, 'Did you pray this morning?' He answered, 'Yes.'

'How long did you pray for?' she queried. 'Half an hour,' the Archbishop replied. 'And what did you say to God in that half hour?' 'Well,' he answered, 'I talked to God for about a minute. But it took me 29 minutes to get there.'

That is the secret. Taking time to let our restless minds quieten, to get in touch with something deep within ourselves, to become aware of God's presence.

19

Quelling the Tempest

If our lives are in turmoil we may feel that there is no way to quieten the din in our mind. But we are wrong. Even though the surface of our lives may be deeply disturbed, there is always a place deep within where there is calm.

Getting in touch with that deeper place takes time. But that is all it takes. A time to be still, to be quiet until the turmoil within begins to ease. If we allow him, Jesus is as willing to quieten the storms in our lives as he was willing to quell the tempest on the Lake of Galilee when his friends battled with an angry sea.

Jesus and his disciples were in a boat, Matthew tells us, when suddenly a storm broke over the lake, so violent that the boat was being swamped by the waves. Jesus was asleep. 'So they went to him and woke him saying, "Save us, Lord, we are lost!" And he said to them, "Why are you so frightened, you who have so little faith?" And then he stood up and rebuked the winds and the sea; and there was a great calm' (Matthew 8:24–27).

Augustine has this advice for those who feel they are being swamped by the storms of life:

For Christians who fear they are
drowning in the world's business
the worst thing they can do is panic.
There can be no question of escape
from the situation;
We are many miles from land
and there is no help near.
The one thing we can do
is to withdraw, as it were,
into ourselves,
to find the Christ within,
who is as powerful
to still the inner tempest
as He was to subdue the waves
on the Lake of Galilee.

Our prayer of silence takes us down to that stillness at the centre of our being, to that innermost self where there is always peace. When we become more quiet we find the peace that is hidden in the depths of our being, but is submerged under the agitation of everyday life.

So, in the words of a beautiful prayer, 'I weave a silence around my lips, my mind, my heart.' The prayer continues with this appeal: 'Calm me, Lord, as you stilled the storm. Still me, Lord, and keep me from harm. Let all the tumult within me cease. Enfold me, Lord, in your peace.'

It is a long way from the surface of our lives, a long road from the troubled mind to the place of peace in the centre of our being. 'The longest road,' wrote Dag Hammarskjöld, 'is the journey inward. Between you and him lie care, uncertainty, doubt.'

To reach the place where Christ awaits us we need to be prepared for long periods of silence and quiet, long enough for our doubts to dissolve, our cares to lose their urgent pressures, our uncertainty to give way to trust. To wait in silence for as long as it takes is to be taken eventually to the still centre where we find that the mind has become quiet and the heart is at peace. And, in the stillness, we find God.

20

'The Womb of Silence'

Our response to the invitation, 'Be still and know that I am God,' is beautifully summed up in the following reflection by an unknown writer.

THE WOMB OF SILENCE

Not in the whirlwind,
not in the lightning,
not in the strife of tongues,
or in the jangling of subtle reasoning
is He to be found,
but in the still small voice
speaking in the womb of silence.
Therefore be silent.

Let the past be silent.
Let there be no vain regrets,
no brooding on past failures,
no bitterness,
no judgment of oneself

or of others.
Let all be silent.

Be still and know.
Be still and look.
Let the eyes of the mind be closed,
that you may hear
what otherwise you would not hear,
that you may know
what otherwise you would not know.

Abandon yourself to Him
in longing love, simply,
holding on to nothing but Him.
So you may enter the silence of eternity
and know the union of yourself with Him.
And if in the silence he does not answer,
He is still there.
His silence is the silence of love.
Wait then in patience
and in submission.
It is good to wait in silence
for His coming.

PART THREE
WE SHALL REST AND WE AND WE SHALL SEE

21

Steeped in Quietness

A short description in Augustine's book *The City of God* offers us, I believe, a perfect model for silent prayer.

In the final paragraph he describes the process, as he sees it, by which we enter into our life with God in eternity.

He writes: 'In eternity we shall rest and we shall see. We shall see and we shall love. We shall love and we shall praise.'

For me, these words suggest the stages by which we also become aware of our union with God in this life.

Our first experience of eternity, he tells us, is as a haven of rest. And resting is the starting point for our journey to our hearts, but it is only the start. In resting we begin the journey that will transform our lives. We shall find a new way of seeing and then a new way of loving. Of loving ourselves, and others, and God.

To spend time resting from all effort prepares us for a living encounter with the Lord. When we come to believe that God is, before all else, the one who invites us to a place of rest, then we will cease our struggling and let him enfold us in his peace.

We no longer wear ourselves out trying to find God, or trying to gain his approval. Instead, we wait for him in silence and peace. We listen, and in the silence we hear his gentle invitation to that quiet place within where he waits for us.

So we bring our body and mind into a state of stillness, that stillness described in Psalm 130 in which all words disappear, in which our whole being is steeped in quietness and trust:

> O Lord, my heart is not proud
> nor haughty my eyes.
> I have not gone after things too great
> nor marvels beyond me.
> Truly I have set my soul
> in silence and peace.
> As a child in its mother's arms
> even so my soul.
> O Israel, hope in the Lord
> both now and for ever.

This is our cue: to rest in the Lord's presence as a child in its mother's arms. It is so simple, and so sensible.

As we are drawn deeper into the silence all sorts of things happen. But to begin with let us first trust the silence, trust that God is at the heart of the silence. In time the silence will deepen. We do not look for anything except to find our way to the still centre where Christ is.

22

Giving Ourselves Permission to Rest

Once, a woman arriving for an eight-day retreat seemed to me to be utterly exhausted. So for her first day she took my advice to sit in the garden and admire the budding blossoms. It was early spring.

The second day came. I asked her to continue to sit in the garden and admire the beauty around her.

On the morning of the third day she looked a bit perplexed when I asked her to do the same.

When we reached the fourth morning she said to me: 'For the first few days I thought I was on a botanical journey. But now I see that I am only just ready to start my retreat properly.'

Her expectation was probably to be plunged into a programme of Scripture reading, spiritual exercises and spiritual direction. But sometimes when we set aside time for the Lord we are in no fit state to settle down to pray.

It is not because we lack goodwill, or because our faith is weak. It is not that there is something in our lives, some moral problem perhaps, coming between us and God. It is simply that we are too anxious, too agitated, too confused. We ignore the signs of heaviness and tiredness and try to get started. Our training has probably conditioned us to plod on no matter how weary the mind and heart may be. No wonder our attempts to pray can so often seem to fail!

When we are exhausted we need to rest. This applies as much to prayer as to our daily living. So we should give ourselves permission to rest.

This is what our silent prayer is all about. We rest in the Lord. We try to be quiet and let the silence speak to us, to be quiet and let the Lord work in us, to be quiet and just enjoy being with him, even if we feel nothing.

Sitting in the priory garden quietly absorbing the sights and sounds of early spring was a perfect way to start a journey into deeper silence.

Now, the invitation to use our prayer time as primarily a time of rest is one our ego will resist. The ego wants to be active, doing, making an effort to show God we are seriously intent on making good use of our time with him. To be invited to sit and rest does not please the ego. It will do anything rather than take a back seat. It will fight every effort on our part to let God 'do the driving'.

So we must be prepared for resistance from within to our plans for our prayer time. The more determined we are to do nothing, the more frustrated our ego becomes and the more it will resist. When, after maybe a long period spent in resting with the Lord, we feel we have achieved nothing, feel it is a waste of time, we can be sure that the ego is urging us to admit failure and give up.

Augustine found 'ego' a problem. 'All the time I wanted to stand and listen. To listen to your voice,' he told God. 'But I could not, because another voice, the voice of my own ego, dragged me away.'

Once we become aware of the wiles of our own ego we shall find it easier to do nothing but rest in the Lord without feeling guilty.

23

'Come to Me'

A few years ago, on the third day of a retreat I was giving, a loud knock on the door of the room set aside for seeing people heralded the arrival of the oldest sister in the community. She wanted 'a few minutes'.

Sitting down, she said: 'I was very cross on the first night. You told us not to read during the retreat and I had brought all the notes from my last retreat in case you were boring. But yesterday I went into the chapel to try to be quiet. I thought I heard the Lord say, "How can I talk to you when you are all over the place?"'

For people trained to exert every effort to lift up mind and heart to God in time of prayer, the invitation to rest might seem a surrender to idleness. To rest from effort seems to deny the value of our faithful attempts to please God.

All our lives, perhaps, we have strained to please God by trying to keep our minds attuned to our words in prayer. We have struggled to ward off stray thoughts. We have failed again and again. But we have gone on believing that we must keep trying. The result so often is a weariness with prayer, a feeling of guilt, or we resign ourselves to simply reciting set prayers.

Of course, no time spent in prayer is ever wasted. Our efforts are always of value. God accepts all our prayers, delighting in the gift we make him of our time.

But he must weep for us as he sees us wear ourselves down by our struggles and exhaust ourselves in our battles to fight the mind's wandering. He must weep for us, too, when we get so discouraged. All he wants from us is to rest in him, and allow him to give us rest for our souls.

There is an important moment in the life of Jesus' disciples when they returned to him after their first attempts to minister in his name and with his power. 'Come apart to a lonely place and rest awhile,' Jesus said to them.

The disciples perhaps would have wanted to talk about their experiences, but he wanted them to rest with him in a place where they could be all alone. This is the offer, the invitation, to us too. To be quiet, at ease with God.

'Come to me all you who are weary and I will give you rest,' says Jesus.

How easy it is for us to miss that invitation.

24

He Closes Our Eyes

Augustine relates in his *Confessions* that long before he accepted Christ and his gospel he was being led into a place of quietness. Looking back years after his conversion he saw that God had been enveloping him in his love, drawing him, unawares, into his embrace. He wrote:

> Unknown to me you caressed my head. You closed my eyes lest they see the things that keep me from you. I lost for a while the heavy burden of self and my madness was lulled to sleep. And when I awoke in you I saw you as utterly different.
>
> (*Confessions* 7.14)

In these simple sentences Augustine lays before us the way in which God draws us into our own place of rest.

God's first action is to enfold our weary heads. The word Augustine uses for caress, or enfold, suggests the image of a bird gathering her young ones under her protecting wings. It is the image Jesus uses when he laments the refusal of the people of Jerusalem to accept his loving protection: 'How often have I longed to gather your children together, as a hen gathers her chicks under her wings, and you refused!' (Matthew 23:37).

God next closes Augustine's eyes lest he be seduced by empty joys. In time of silent prayer God closes our eyes, too, lest we be drawn aside into all that keeps us from the way of peace.

Augustine then discovers that, for a moment, he forgets about himself. His greatest burden, he sees, is the heavy burden of self. 'I beg you, O Lord my God,' he writes, 'to look upon me and listen to me. Have pity on me and heal me, for you see that I have become a problem to myself, and this is the sickness from which I suffer.'

This is the burden that is lifted for us, too, when we come before God in silence. We forget ourselves. We forget for a while all that crushes us. Self-forgetfulness is one of the great blessings of silent prayer. To lose the burden of self and rest in God's love is a pearl of great price. Even more so is the promise that our madness is lulled to sleep.

Augustine discovered that his troubled surface self was calmed and healed, and he found the peace which surpasses all expectations. Out of this state he awakens. Not an awakening into the hard reality of everyday life, but awakening with a new vision.

Augustine saw God in a completely new light. And in seeing God he saw everything differently.

25

Bill's Taizé Experience

In our deep resting with the Lord we, too, have the experience of awakening with a cleansed and healed vision. We see in a way that we have never seen before. We come to realise how unaware we have been.

In ordinary life we are blind to much of what goes on in our lives and in the world around us. We live in a dazed state, as Bill discovered on a visit to Taizé.

Bill, who was a member of our community for six years and then left, told me what happened to him when, shortly after leaving us, he experienced the long silence during the evening prayer of the monastery. In Taizé worship, people are lulled into silence by the repetition of a few simple words chanted by the brothers and the congregation.

'After 45 minutes, the chant was only just beginning to penetrate the hard little shell we carry around with us,' Bill told me as we walked in the Clent Hills. 'Something within was beginning to waken up. Like someone rousing from deep slumber, coming to consciousness, I came out after nearly three hours in that prayer and felt it was only just beginning to get through. I realised that I would have to do this every day for it to have an effect. And yet I could have talked about prayer with anyone!

'It was all about being still and letting something happen. To let the prayer erode the resistance you put up without realising it. And you had to resist trying to understand what was going on, and articulating it and sharing it. The more I stayed there, the more the chant washed over me, the more it began to break through to me.

'As I woke I prayed, babbled like a child. But as consciousness returned, I could not hold on to the child's prayer. I realised that my ordinary, everyday self seemed to exist in a kind of coma.' TRANCE

26

Patient Waiting

How long we spend resting in the Lord before our vision clears can sometimes depend on how harassed or weary we are when we come to pray. For most of us the time needed in our modern world is long, longer than we believe.

Some years ago I learned the value of being prepared to wait for a very long time. I was then working in Birmingham. For my day off I usually travelled down to Herefordshire. This time, it was at the end of the August bank holiday. As I drove along the A146 I met long lines of traffic heading back to Birmingham. The drone of cars and motorbikes increased my weariness.

Arriving at the little cottage in Lower Hardwick where I was to spend 24 hours I prepared a simple supper and afterwards sat out happily at the back of the cottage to read the papers as the sun moved down the sky.

I soon became aware that my mind was not absorbing what I was reading. So I put the newspaper aside and decided to catch up on my prayers. Again, my mind failed to respond. To focus was painful. Laying aside my prayer book I surrendered to the peace of the evening and decided to spend the time with the Lord quietly in silence.

The time passed slowly. The main feeling was one of weariness, of stupor. Why continue? Go to bed, my good sense suggested. Yet I felt that staying on there in the silence was the best thing I could do. So I stayed, and an hour passed. My exhaustion had begun to lift.

Again, good sense suggested that now was the moment to head for sleep. But some instinct kept me there in the garden seat that overlooked the spacious fields, with the cattle sheltering under the trees and the Black Mountains fading.

Time passed quickly now. An hour later I was as fresh as if I had enjoyed a full night's sleep. My eyes took in everything before me. No longer did I look without seeing. Now I saw the things my tired eyes had failed to notice. Each object seemed to be bathed in its own individual glory. Each thing seemed holy. The sound from the sparrows in the eaves was a welcome sound. The rustle of the leaves was soothing. Each moment seemed filled with a presence.

That experience taught me that to find rest through silence in God's presence may sometimes take longer than we imagine when we set out on the road to silent prayer. But the effect of spending a long time in silent resting with the Lord is that our weariness dissolves, our vision that was clouded and unseeing is cleared, and we see with new eyes. As our mind becomes quiet, our inner eye is opened. We are in a new world.

27

'Everything Looked Different'

Silent prayer is there for everyone /It appeals to all ages. Once, *& for ever* when giving a retreat in North Wales, I was asked by the sister in charge if I would talk to the young people who were connected with the community. 'I hope you don't mind, Father,' she explained, 'but I have invited all the youngsters to come for you to talk to them on Sunday afternoon.'

When they arrived, they were aged between ten and 22. Thomas, the ten-year-old, looked bewildered. James, the 22-year-old, a postgraduate student at the university, looked faintly put out. I did not know what I could say to such a diverse group, so I said: 'Let's go down to the chapel and have some quiet prayer.'

For half an hour I tried to lead them into centring prayer, as the prayer of silence and stillness is sometimes known. The two 15-year-old boys on the back pew giggled most of the time, but the others were quite serious.

After we finished, as they came out of the silence, I asked them how they felt. Two of the replies struck me. One girl of about 16 said: 'When I was coming here this afternoon I was worried about certain things that are happening in my life. When we finished the prayer I felt I was no longer worried about them.'

Another girl in her early teens said: 'When we came down here to the chapel I looked around. I had never seen it before. Then we went into the silence, and when I opened my eyes again everything around me looked different.'

On another occasion, when I was a parish priest, a family asked me to come and have a word with their 11-year-old son Michael, who was suffering from a lot of bullying at his school.

After we had talked for a while I asked if he would like to have a little time of quiet prayer. We sat for 20 minutes, handed everything over to the Lord, and allowed the lovely peace of the room and the garden outside to bring us to stillness.

I still have a vivid picture of that quiet room and Michael sitting so calmly and saying, 'I think the room looks different and I feel everything is going to be all right.'

28

As Simple As a Child

A young friend of mine, a busy teacher, explained in a letter how he had struggled for many years to find the 'right' way to pray, and how silent prayer came as a great shock because of its total simplicity. He discovered there is no special method. 'It is about disciplining oneself to remain still – and open to God.'

In his childhood Mark had a very simple faith. 'I believed that God created me and cared for me. From my grandmother I saw how it was possible to simply "be" in God's loving presence. As I grew older it no longer seemed enough. I wanted to "do" more, saying prayers and trying various methods of devotional prayer.

'Only recently have I returned to my original, childhood method of prayer and found the healing I had never thought possible before. I feel as simple as a child.'

The practicalities of silent prayer are straightforward, but everyone will find his or her own approach, says Mark. 'I find it helpful before beginning my time of silence to say the opening words of the Hail Mary, up to the word "Jesus". I let the holy name linger. However, when I pray, I use no words. Silent prayer is not about delighting in images or language. It is about leaving aside all that is familiar. No safety nets.

'Instead of praying *for* someone, or about a particular situation, one holds these before God open-handed, believing that God will deal with that person or that situation however he sees fit. It is based solely on trust. It is also about learning to take God at his word and believing he will dwell within us whether we are personally good or not. God is present within me, even if I do not "feel" his presence. This is especially important when distracting thoughts fizz around in my head and I cannot find the stillness I seek.

'Sometimes, I may only have five minutes of the allotted 20 in any kind of silence. When I am full of distractions, I remind myself that God is within me and that kernel of "me" is enjoying his presence, beneath the surface and its disturbances. Gradually, I slip the anchor down into that place of deep silence and allow the roaring waters to have their storming out.

'There is no "getting it right" involved, which is a relief after years of battling, of visualising biblical scenes and re-enacting them with love, penitence or devotion. Now I fast from images, from feelings, from penitent tears and holy aspirations. I delight in finding God exactly where he is, and leaving him free within me to accomplish whatever he wishes.

'I have stopped wanting to be someone else – a better Catholic, for example. Instead I have started to discover my "Mark-ness", the true image of me which was within me from the moment of my baptism.

'For me, the heart of silent prayer is the discovery that we are called to be ourselves, our true selves, in the presence of the Trinity, helping God to work within the world.'

29

Just Be There

The prayer of silence and stillness is widely promoted as a cure for modern life's frenzy. And it may be that this is what first draws us to it. But as we grow to love this form of prayer, it is not for its side effects that we persevere. After a time we come to this prayer with only one desire – to come into the presence of the living God. We seek our still centre not to find inner peace for its own sake, but to find God.

We let go of ideas about what we are supposed to achieve. We rest in the Lord, stay quiet, so that we can be in his presence without seeking anything. We lay down our burdens, our problems. We let go, and let God carry us. At first this does not seem anything like prayer. Yet we are prepared to go along with it.

We find after a time that we no longer seek God's gifts, his graces, no longer ask for anything, or expect anything. We leave self behind.

Our relationship with God changes, from wanting things from him to simply being with him, with no other motive. 'If you keep asking God to do things for you, your time of prayer is one prolonged ego trip,' John Main said. 'You become more deeply hooked into yourself. To gain freedom of spirit you must be unhooked from your own self-conscious preoccupations.'

Of course, we are used to seeing God as the giver of gifts. The idea that we can have a relationship with him in which we ask for nothing and nothing is given is very rare and very liberating. Augustine teaches us: 'Do not wish to ask anything of God except God. Love him without seeking gain. Desire Him alone.' This is how to love God *gratis*, without seeking gain, he says: 'To hope for God from God, to wish to be filled with God, to be satiated by him.'

Meister Eckhart wrote: 'When I pray for nothing, then I pray rightly, and that prayer is proper and powerful. I never pray so well as when I pray for nothing and for nobody.'

Father Pedro Arrupe, a past superior general of the Jesuit Order, told the story of a young pupil of his whom he met when he worked on the missions. She would spend hours on end kneeling in the chapel, close to the tabernacle.

'She would arrive in the chapel, and walking with the peculiar silence of those who are used to walking barefoot and noiseless from childhood, she would get as close to the Lord as her respect would allow her, and there she would kneel, indifferent to all that surrounded her.'

One day they met as she was leaving. 'We began to talk and little by little I turned the subject of our conversation towards her visits to the altar,' Father Arrupe wrote. 'At an opportune moment I asked her: "What do you do for such a long time at the altar?" Without hesitation, as if she had thought out her reply long before, she answered, "Nothing." "How do you mean, nothing?" I insisted. "Do you think it is really possible to kneel there for so long and do nothing?"

'The precision of my question, which removed all possibility of ambiguity, seemed to disconcert her a little. She was not prepared for this kind of interrogation, and she took longer in replying. At last she opened her lips: "What do I do before Jesus? Well ... be there!" she explained. And she fell silent again. It would seem to a superficial mind that she had said very little. But in reality she had said everything.'

Into those few words, Father Arrupe saw, was condensed the whole truth of all those endless hours spent near the altar. 'Hours of friendship. Hours of intimacy, in which nothing is asked and nothing is given. One is just there.'

30

Watching What God is Doing

The kind of spirituality and prayer many of us have been used to is concerned with making things happen, asking God to do things for us, trying to do things for God. Our prayer of stillness is all about being with God without any agenda. It is about just being there.

We no longer have to see our spiritual life as a kind of battleground where we exert ourselves to combat our faults, or to attain the good qualities we associate with living the gospel. Nor do we have to strive to come closer to God. Our starting place is not here. As we have learnt from Augustine, the starting point is in resting, in finding the place of rest within. And from this place of rest we watch what God is doing for us now and has done in the past.

We focus on what God is showing us and we watch our reactions. It is an exciting adventure. As God sheds light into our hearts we resist trying to understand, or to make sense of our lives. That will come later. As we become quieter, as we learn *how* to watch, how to observe patiently and with compassion, we become aware of what is going on.

In the silence we know we have a choice. We do not have to be at the mercy of our thoughts and feelings. We let our thoughts come and let them pass on. We remain still and observe our feelings. We become detached.

It is a crucial turning point when, instead of being tossed around by our thoughts and feelings, we stay and watch them, refusing now to go chasing every stray thought, or being dragged away by every stray feeling.

We watch our thoughts as if we were standing at a window and they were passing along on the other side of the street. We observe them, distance ourselves from them, and just label them: anger, say, obsession, or resentment. It is totally different from introspection, which is the ruin of silent prayer. We become observers, rather than players in the games that are going on inside.

Even good thoughts, spiritual thoughts, that come to us are meant to be gently put aside. This is not the time for any thinking whatsoever. It is a time to rest from all effort, except the effort to remain still. We are just sitting, in touch with the present moment and taking stock of where we are. There is no tomorrow, no yesterday. There is just the present moment, and we rest in it.

While we are sitting, simply experiencing the present, experiencing the chair we are sitting on, listening to the sounds on the road outside, we begin to observe our mind and its movements. We are wide awake, watching, more alive than when we are dragged along by our fears, our anxieties, our fantasies.

We stay alert, receptive, and keep ourselves from daydreaming or drowsing off into sleep. Jesus told his disciples, 'Wait here and stay awake with me' (Matthew 26:38).

For a few moments we come into the present. Our vision has altered. Our perception of everything changes. We see how things really are.

PART FOUR
DISCOVERING OUR TRUE SELVES

31

Seeing With New Eyes

Christine, a friend of mine, was introduced to silent prayer during a retreat in Wales at the age of 40 plus. Some time after returning home, she realised she was seeing herself and her life with new eyes.

'The first thing that became clearer to me,' said Christine, 'was that, although I really did want a closer relationship with God, I was actually quite afraid of one.'

It was a fear of 'being taken over' and becoming a stranger, she said. Would she lose something of herself, or be asked to give up things that now seemed important to her happiness?

'By the end of the retreat,' she went on, 'I was beginning to see that the Lord is not an entity outside myself, with whom I have to reconcile all the forces within my personality, but is somehow in the deepest part of myself. There is no real conflict between all that makes me what I am, and God. The problem is that I don't really understand what my real self is, and haven't therefore allowed it to grow.'

Another major change was in Christine's way of looking at how the Lord works in our lives. Initially, the texts given her for prayer time during the retreat were about God's fatherly love. It seemed a long time since she had felt that!

Recent years had not been happy ones. Struggling with the failing health of parents, for example, Christine had to abandon holiday plans three years in succession and seemed unable to find any way of recharging her batteries.

'It sounds childish,' she acknowledged, 'but I suppose I expected God to intervene in some way, just to give me the chance to get on top of things, and yet the more I felt I needed his support and presence the further away he seemed.'

By the middle of the week, unwinding in the peace and silence, she was able to see it was not so much what had or had not happened in her life that got her down, but what she called her response of inertia and self-pity.

'One of the prayer texts I was given was from Deuteronomy: "I set before you life or death." And I realised that on so many occasions I had chosen death.

'In the stillness I began to see that God works mainly not by manipulating circumstances and events to our advantage in response to our faith and petitions. Rather, a growing relationship with him in prayer gives us the strength to change the circumstances that can be changed, or to accept those we cannot, and to trust he will give us the necessary support.

'I also began to see "sin" not as transgressions against the commandments, but as all the forces within me that deaden me, and make me negative and lacking in hope. And that the salvation Christ brings is not appeasement of his angry Father, but his ability to heal me and free me from all these negative forces.

'My life had been handed back to me, to be lived in union with the Lord who is within me, and whom I could find and grow closer to if I made sufficient time to rest with him in prayer.'

32

Lord, Who Am I?

To see ourselves and how our mind behaves can be the beginning of a new life. It can be daunting, too. In the silence, maybe for the first time in my life I am observing my thoughts instead of being dragged along by them. I am standing back from my thoughts and seeing how I am bullied by them. The sight is not always a pretty one.

A student at a week's retreat, a week of total silence, had declared himself an agnostic. During the daily six hours of prayer he made what he said was an amazing discovery. He became aware for the first time in his life how wholly negative his thoughts were. But once his eyes had been opened to his negativity he was delighted: he could begin to deal with it.

It is quite a shock for us to discover how self-centred our own thoughts are, and how negative they can be, especially about ourselves. Now, this was not what I expected from prayer. Here was I expecting to find God and his peace, but what do I find? I first find myself.

And this discovery is my great hope. For as soon as I begin to see how negative and self-obsessed my thinking is I begin to be able to stand back from it. Not immediately, perhaps not for a long time, but this is a first step in being freed from it.

The great new adventure that opens up to us is that 'I am about to know myself in order to forget myself,' as John Main put it.

Our journey inwards, as it was for Augustine, is from our mind and its self-centredness, its self-fixation, to the centre, to our heart. It is a journey into self-discovery and a journey into God.

While we are immersed in our daily lives, most of us are barely conscious of what we are thinking. But when I sit in God's presence I begin to see that I have lived most of my life running away from myself. Losing myself in activities, in work, in diversion, I have lived outside myself. As Augustine pointed out, we become strangers to ourselves. We do not recognise ourselves.

The most important search in life for each one of us, he tells us, is to know God and to know ourselves. He would say that to know God one has first to know oneself. His constant cry was 'Lord, that I may know myself that I may know you.'

And Francis of Assisi in his long nights of prayer in the cave at Averna would repeat over and over again the questions, 'Lord, who am I? Lord, who are you?'

In *The New Man,* Thomas Merton writes that unless we discover our deep self, which is hidden with Christ in God, we will never know ourselves as persons. 'Nor will we know God. For it is by the door of this deep self that we enter into the spiritual knowledge of God.'

33

The Teacher Within

Augustine would tell us that we have all we need for our spiritual journey because we have within us the greatest of all teachers, Christ himself. 'Christ lives in the heart of each one of us, and he is our best teacher,' he writes. 'I, the preacher, am pouring a torrent of words into your ears. My words are meaningless unless he who dwells within you reveals their sense to you.

'Your true teacher will always be the teacher within. It is he who enables you to understand, in the depths of your being, the truth of what is said to you.'

In his commentary on John's Gospel he explains: 'God speaks to us within. He speaks to us in our inner self when we are attentive to him. Without words he instructs us in silence, drenching our souls with the light of understanding. He stirs in us an eager longing for the beautiful intimacy of his presence within. But it is through our daily practice that we become capable of this intimacy. It is by walking with him that we grow, by going forward that we walk, so that we may reach the goal' *(Tract 54* 8.12.44–50).

It is a major step in our spiritual life to discover the teacher within and to want to learn from him alone. This teacher forms us in a way that no other teacher can do.

So in our time of silence we remain still and keep ourselves present to him in an attitude of loving receptivity. We remain constantly attentive, knowing that God, who dwells in the depths of our being, is always doing great things.

Out of our resting comes the vision of how our lives might change. Out of our openness comes the willingness to conform to what God's spirit prompts us to do.

Dr E. F. Schumacher, the author of *Small is Beautiful*, was in his forties when he travelled to Burma as an economic adviser to the UN. At the time he was an agnostic, he said, without any spiritual roots, a typical Western intellectual.

While he was there he was struck by the air of calmness people there carried about with them. He knew that many of them at some stage in their lives spent time in a Buddhist monastery learning to be still. So he decided to try to learn about the routine of monastic silence. He cancelled his engagements and took himself off for five weeks to a Buddhist monastery. Those five weeks proved a turning point.

At first Dr Schumacher found it physically difficult to sit still. Once he achieved that, he found his emotions stopped running away with him. Next he found his heart became quiet. Finally, as a result, his mind became clear, and this surprised him. He had always supposed himself to be clear-minded.

He now realised that in the past his mind had been obscured by the ever-shifting clouds of his restless desires. And it was out of this new clarity of mind that he saw his spiritual path being revealed to him. He became a Catholic and was regarded as one of the most influential thinkers of the twentieth century.

34

The Eye of the Heart

When we were young novices the obligation to keep silence at meals or between certain hours, and the great silence after night prayers until morning recreation, seemed a kind of restriction, a penance. How little we understood the great value of silence!

The aim of keeping silent while we pray is so that our minds become still and our hearts awaken. It is as if our hearts are usually in a kind of trance. While the mind is processing a million thoughts and words the heart remains numb.

If we could, as it were, put a blindfold around the eyes of the mind while we are communing with God we would be forced to develop that faculty which can really communicate with him, our heart. And if our heart were awake, alert, we would find ourselves continually drawn towards God.

For this to happen we need to clear the dross, the debris which clogs the heart, the vast number of words, thoughts and fantasies that constantly get between us and God while we are trying to be with him.

Seeing with the heart is a rare gift. Talkers and thinkers greatly outnumber those who can see properly. 'The mind has a thousand eyes, the heart but one,' writes the poet Bouillon. In our silent prayer the thousand eyes of the mind are closed and the eye of the heart is opened.

To see only with the eyes of the mind is to be misled by our prejudices, our fears, our anxieties. To see with the eye of the heart is to see clearly. This is surely what Shakespeare had in mind when he wrote, 'We worldly men have miserable, mad, mistaking eyes' (*Titus Andronicus* Act V, Scene iv).

Resting in the Lord is the way by which the weary eye of the heart is cleansed and refreshed. We begin to see from somewhere deep within. We see with the inner eye, the eye of wisdom, the eye of love. We realise what Jesus meant when he said, 'If your eye is sound, your whole body will be full of light' (Matthew 6:22). Augustine goes so far as to say: 'Our whole task in life is to heal the eye of the heart so that God may be seen.'

What happens when our vision is changed happens without any effort on our part. Once the eye of the heart is opened then we see God.

And we see the beauty and the wonder of the world.

But first of all, we begin to see our true selves, our own beauty and who we really are.

35

God Loves Us

'Real isn't how you are made,' said the Skin Horse in Margery Williams' book, *The Velveteen Rabbit*. 'It's a thing that happens to you. When a child loves you for a long, long time,' he continued, 'not just to play with, but *really* loves you, then you become Real.'

Everyone needs to know that they are loved. In our journey through life the greatest discovery of all is that we are loved by God. Only that love makes us completely Real.

The truth is that God loves us and calls us his beloved. But our lives are often so busy that we no longer give ourselves the chance to hear him say 'I love you.'

But some have a problem in accepting, in really believing or feeling, that God loves them. Jo, a regular visitor to our priory, tells me that she remembers the moment, in her thirties, when she first heard this message. She had grown up at a time when the fear of God was preached more than God's love, with the result that 'many of us were afraid of God, of being watched and judged, and threatened with God's punishment.'

Jo tells me that she went to Mass one day in West London and heard the youngish Irish priest say this: 'Most of you have come here to live and work in London from different parts of the country and from all over the world, and when you come to this church you feel anonymous. You think nobody knows you and what has happened to you in your life, or what sins you may have committed. But God knows.'

At this point, Jo said, her heart sank. But after a pause the priest continued: 'And God knows why your life has been as it is, and he loves you.'

This was not what she expected to hear thirty years ago. Most members of the congregation, even the young, would have been waiting for what usually came next, the condemnation or the pep talk. 'To be told that God knows everything about us and our circumstances, and that he loves us because of everything, not even in spite of everything, was a revelation.'

Sitting in silence allows God to wipe away our fear and our feeling of unworthiness. Gradually we become aware that the love God has for us is very real and that he loves us and cares for us just as we are.

'You care for each one of us as if we were the only one you had to care for. Yet you care for all of us as if we were the only one' (*Confessions* 3.11).

36

The Fruitful Vine

When Jesus spoke of himself on the night before he died as the true vine in his Father's vineyard, he promised to abide with us and to nourish us. He told his disciples: 'I am the vine and you are the branches. Whoever remains in me, with me in him, bears fruit in plenty' (John:15:5).

In our time of silent waiting we are allowing the sap, the life that flows in the vine, to flow through the branches. We are not seeking union with God. We already have that. Our task is to remain close to him and enjoy that union.

'It is not that God comes to us, as if he were absent,' Augustine reminds us, 'or even that we "go" to him. God is always present to us but we, like blind people, do not have the eyes to see him.'

In order to see God we have to enter a new relationship with him, enter into a new place. 'It was in my inmost heart,' wrote Augustine, 'it was there, Lord, that you made me begin to love you, and you made me glad at heart' (*Confessions* 9.4).

The awareness of our union with the life-giving vine, the unknown sweetness that we find in our inmost heart, is not achieved without a struggle. It is a struggle between our surface self, the person on show to the world, and our deeper self.

It is what Paul, in one of his letters to the Christians in Rome, describes as the split between our spiritual and our unspiritual self. It is the conflict between the ego and what he calls 'my true self'.

Thomas Merton writes that the aim of being still before God is 'to set free the divine light which is mysteriously present and shining in each of us, although it is enveloped in an insidious web of the psyche's weaving.'

This divine light is trapped in a web which our unspiritual self – to use Paul's words – weaves around it. If we are to release that light and let it shine we have to free it from the tangled web we have wrapped it in.

In the struggle to discard the shell that life has created, or we have created, grace is working gently if painfully, inviting our true self to emerge from the womb into the fullness of life.

Our hours of prayer open us up to our deeper self. In that stillness we find the true self created in God's image that life's cares and sorrows and sins can never destroy.

We discover, like Augustine, that we are waking with a new vision. Our priorities are changing. Our fears are assuaged and our anxieties lessened.

We shall also find, as promised, that we have everything within us for our spiritual journey: the source of life, the wisdom we need.

Deep down we find our basic sanity and basic goodness.

We discover our own deepest self.

37

Streams of Living Water

Many people wanting to make spiritual progress, wanting to know God and his love, fall into the trap of starting from the outside and working inwards, beginning with outer virtues and hoping little by little to change within. But for Augustine change has to be from inside out.

He writes: 'At the well where Our Lord sat down to rest great mysteries took place.' He was referring to the time when Jesus was making his way back to Galilee at the end of his ministry in Judaea. Tired by the journey, Jesus sat down by Jacob's well. A Samaritan woman came to draw water and Jesus told her, 'Whoever drinks this water will be thirsty again, but no one who drinks the water that I shall give will ever be thirsty again: the water I shall give will become a spring of water within, welling up for eternal life' (John 4:13–14).

At another time, after teaching in the temple at Jerusalem, Jesus said: 'Let anyone who is thirsty come to me! Let anyone who believes in me come and drink. As scripture says, "From his heart shall flow streams of living water"' (John 7:37–38).

That is the pledge. We shall drink from the stream of living water within. Gradually this will lead to growth and transformation in our lives. It all has to happen within, and God is working in us and with us to achieve it.

In the early stages of our quiet prayer we begin to discover the areas of our lives where the streams of living water which Jesus offers have turned into stagnant pools. We may find ourselves asking: 'Have I always been so angry and just never noticed it?' Or, like the student, 'Have I always lived with these negative thoughts?'

So our first discovery in the deeper silence may be our own stagnation, created by attitudes we have not noticed in ourselves before. There may be unacknowledged depression, fear or anger, for example, which can all create stagnation. There is no need to be alarmed. Once these are recognised we can deal with them, and the life-giving water begins to flow again, bit by bit.

Over the years we have trained ourselves to stop the stream of life from flowing. We have created our whirlpools and defended them. It takes time to see our defensiveness. Patience and time spent in the Lord's healing presence helps us to see our manoeuvres more clearly. It may be unpleasant, but it is also a bit like taking huge draughts of fresh air.

Stuart, the young man in Iris Murdoch's novel *The Good Apprentice* who aims at holiness, prefers the way of meditation to what he has been taught was prayer. Prayer, he believed, was 'struggle, reflection, self-examination', whereas meditation, he felt, was 'refuge, quietness, purification, replenishment'.

Silence purifies, silence empties. By taking refuge in the silence and allowing our minds and hearts to become quiet, the stagnant pools will be freed and the stream of living water will flow again from the depths of our being.

38

Compassion

What are we supposed to do with the faults and failings we begin to recognise in ourselves during our silent prayer – our jealousy, say, our impatience, our tendency to judge? Silence gives us the confidence to look at the shadow side of our lives, and the parable of the wheat and the darnel in Matthew's Gospel helps to answer this question.

The field of our lives yields both weeds and healthy crops, good qualities and bad; darnel springs up among the wheat. If we follow the advice in the Gospel we would not be eager to root out the weeds. Jesus says, 'Let them grow' (Matthew 13:30).

If we can live with our faults, and not take a sledge-hammer to them, they can be of use to us. If we do not recoil and run away from them, if we can let them be, then we can learn a great deal.

'Be compassionate just as your Father is compassionate,' Jesus told the crowds. 'Do not judge, and you will not be judged; do not condemn, and you will not be condemned; forgive, and you will be forgiven' (Luke 6:36–38). How important it is for us to look on ourselves, as well as on others, with such compassion.

When, instead of hating myself for my faults, I learn to be compassionate towards my own weaknesses, then I will learn to be

ing of the weaknesses of others. The more intolerant
failures and faults, the more intolerant I will be of
ailings.

a licence to be indifferent to our faults, to be self-
to behave just as we like. No. It is a way of treating our
nesses not with severity and hatred, but seeing them as aids, to
teach us patience and compassion, tolerance and understanding. If I
can learn this balance, if I can hold the goodness and weakness of my
life in this way, then my relationships with others will flourish.

Being too severe with our weaknesses leaves us feeling guilty,
with a low sense of our worth. And that means we are no good to
others. It leaves us paralysed. So much good is left undone, not
because of lack of goodwill but because we feel unworthy, useless.

The kingdom of God is about building relationships – a healthy
relationship with ourselves first, then healthy relationships with
others and so with God. If I can be compassionate towards my own
failings, as he is compassionate, then this tolerance and understanding will naturally flow towards others. I shall become a compassionate person. I shall be building his kingdom.

God knows our faults and he loves us. He will take care of them.
It is not the weeds in our lives that God is interested in. He is
interested in the wheat, which he will gather into his barn. Our weeds
he will tie in bundles and throw into the fire.

'Do not abandon your gifts,' Augustine prayed. 'Do not desert
the field in which you have sown the seed, until your harvest is stored
in the heavenly barn.'

39

Buried Hurt

In the silence we may become aware of how much we feel, in some way or other, we are 'victims'.

Of course we have all in some way been the victims of other people's anger, of their selfishness, of their ignorance. We may feel that schoolfriends, teachers or colleagues, or possibly our families have done us harm, have destroyed our confidence. Buried hurts may have lain in our hearts unattended for years. They rise to the surface when we are quiet.

So in our prayer we may become aware of having suffered injustice. And we are upset about it. That is the first stage. The second is working with the feelings that come out of that awareness – our anger, our desire to get even, our resentment, our withdrawal, our coldness.

When we examine the past we tend to find scapegoats and blame others for our problems. But as we learn to sit in the Lord's presence we face these hurts and begin to discover how to leave the past in God's hands. Instead of blaming, we learn in the silence to accept the past with all its brokenness. We accept ourselves, our situation, all our confusion, dislocation and damage. We submit it quietly, and with compassion for ourselves, to the Lord. And we hear him say, 'Do not be afraid. I am with you.'

In the silence we also begin to see not only how we have been victims and how this has determined our thinking and our actions but, more importantly, we start to see how we have sacrificed or manipulated others.

And when our sorrow begins to be as great for what we have done to others as for what has been done to us, then our prayer is deepening. We cannot wipe out the past, but we will try to atone for what we have done.

Becoming aware of our feelings is not an opening for self-criticism, or an invitation to introspection or to brooding over the past. What we find ourselves being led into is a sincere regret for past failings. But the focus of our thoughts is more and more on the sufferings of others. When our attention is focused on our own sorrows, often we are unable to respond to the suffering of others. But in the quietness we begin to see that we have a choice about how we relate to them.

One of the characters in a George Eliot novel sums up his ambition in life with words that could be useful for all of us. He says: 'I will try to make life less bitter for a few within my reach.'

We can start to ease the suffering of those closest to us when we move out of our bitter thoughts about the past and just begin to be here with the present moment, the present reality and its opportunities.

40

Troubling Thoughts

But what are we to do if, in the silence, deeper hurts and fears come to the surface and persist, in spite of our efforts to ignore them? Things that shock. Things we do not like about ourselves.

Our instinct, of course, is to push down the terrors, bury them again in the hidden recesses of our minds. We feel we cannot face them. We pick up something to read, or we get up to do something.

That is probably how we have always dealt with these hurtful memories. But it is possible to deal with them in another way. We have a choice. We can say, 'No. I don't want to go over all this.' And that, at times, may be the best thing to do. But perhaps the fact that these old sorrows are coming to the surface means that the time for healing has come.

With a little faith and courage we can allow painful memories to be exposed to the healing presence of the Lord. The childhood cruelties, neglect or abuse. The hurts we have suffered in life. The rejections, the ridicule, the injustices. These can all be exposed to the rays of healing that come from God's presence each time we place ourselves before him.

You alone will know whether or not the time has come to allow these memories to surface. We can be certain that the Lord wan heal us, and sitting quietly in his presence is the first step towards that healing.

When Jeremiah's enemies decided to do away with him they threw him into the well, letting him down with ropes. 'There was no water in the well, only mud, and into the mud Jeremiah sank' (Jeremiah 38:6). That is how we may feel, not conscious now of the living water that Jesus promised, but that we are sinking in the mud and the mire.

The psalmist says, 'You hide those who trust in you in the shelter of your presence.' For 'hide' we might read 'heal'. To sit with our buried hurts and pain in the presence of the Lord is to allow ourselves to be healed by him. We no longer become involved in trying to sort them out, nor do we recoil from them. We let them be. We sit quietly. We are beginning to have the confidence to outstare our ghosts.

Sometimes when people meditate or pray without words they are accused of trying to anaesthetise themselves to deaden their pain. But what we really do in our quiet prayer is face the pain, engage with it, and transform it into energy for loving.

A passage in John O'Donoghue's book *Divine Beauty* speaks of turning our pain into beauty and compassion. Here is what he writes: 'It is a wonderful day in the life when one is finally able to stand before the long, deep mirror of one's own reflection and view oneself with forgiveness, with appreciation, with acceptance. Most woundedness remains hidden, lost inside forgotten silence. Indeed in s some wound that continues to weep secretly, even empted healing. Where woundedness can be refined onderful transfiguration takes place. Compassion is oundedness.'

to

41

Healing of Memories

Once, at a Charismatic conference in Manchester, we were offered the opportunity for the healing of memories. The Jesuit who was leading the conference invited us to revisit our most painful memories of the past and to try to imagine Jesus as present in each of them.

As he guided us through all the stages of our lives, from childhood on, we were encouraged to bring Jesus into each memory. We were encouraged to recognise that he was not there as a judge, but as one who took on himself all our suffering.

Around me people started to weep, while I sat there as cold as ice. But it was different when, weeks later, I tried this approach on my own. Imagining Jesus present and taking on himself the pain of each situation was the start of being freed from the memories that hurt most. Maybe nothing dramatic, all at once, but it was the beginning.

In our time of prayer we are not delving for our darkest memories, or brooding over them when they come. But we no longer have to shut them out. Being able to sit in silence even if all hell breaks loose is the way to healing. So, if we can, we allow ourselves to imagine those scenes in our past which cause us pain, and see the Lord present in them.

We might think that to see Jesus as present at some of those times would cause us shame or discomfort. Instead, we see those incidents in a very different way. Full of pain, certainly. But now we see Jesus suffering with us.

We know that he was there, then, at the moments we most needed him, though we were unaware of his presence. And we know that he is here, now, gently rescuing us and freeing us from guilt and hurt and fear.

Healing is a slow and painful process but it is liberating. We are being freed from the tyranny of our self-destructive thoughts.

As we let the resentment and hurts of the past be healed and taken from us we shed so much of the self that we have built up and carried like an enormous burden on our backs. We become the self that has not been damaged by the sad experiences of life, the deeper self that remains at all times united with God.

And the more we shed of our past and our baggage, the more that true self radiates its light and its life. The true self is waiting to be born if we can let go of the burdens of the years, the burdens the Lord wants to remove.

As I wait in the silence, I trust that God is leading me to the very depths of my being, enabling me to recover my real, deeper self and to grow to my full potential.

'Stop being who you were, and become who you are,' Paulo Coelho urges.

42

Facing Our Shadows

The search for the real self is central to our journey, wrote Daniel O'Leary. And finding our real self means we have to face our shadows. 'In facing one's shadows, one begins to know truly the light of one's soul.'

'We resist the call into our own mystery,' he writes, 'our own depths. We fear further hurt by unknown demons in the barren places. We rightly suspect that our wounds are deeper than we think – and often hitched to each other all the way back to childhood. It truly is the uncomfortable place we would rather not go. But something tells us it is necessary.'

And he quotes Henri Nouwen, the Dutch priest, who tells us we must live our wounds through instead of thinking them through. 'It is better to feel your wounds deeply than to understand them, to let them into your silence. You need to let your wounds go down into your heart. Then you can live them through and discover that they will not destroy you. Your heart is greater than your wounds.'

'Instead,' says Father O'Leary, 'we cover the hurts of our hearts with the bandages of the mind. We bury our painful emotions and think that they are dead. We forget that our presence and personalities are profoundly influenced and shaped by these underground and often violent realities. We live and act out of the invisible shadow-world that turns silently, within us. Pain needs light. Nothing heals in the dark.'

We grow by dying, he writes, 'There is no other way. In this dying we recognise the false face we've grown used to, the daily lies we tell, the thoughts and deception that crowd our minds, the infidelities we do not commit only because we might get caught, the lovelessness of our lives parading as shallow compassion, our collusion with conformity, our fear of beauty and big dreams.'

We die to self, he says, when we sacrifice the ego of our vanity for the essence of our truest being. 'This is the dying that daily scrapes the self-renewing fat of pride from the ribs of our soul, bringing a fearless inner lightness and clarity. When the eye is unblocked, the Buddhists tell us, the vision is sure.

'This is the liberating dying that puts the truth in our eyes, the resonance in our voice, the power in our presence, the depth in our listening. Since we are now all connected up inside, our heart is no longer divided. Rinsed and cauterised, all that is unauthentic is zapped from our infected being. When the small gods go, God arrives. Heaven, in the end, is where we belong.'

PART FIVE
GOD HEALS OUR BROKENNESS

43

Thinking No Thoughts

Salley Vickers' novel, *Miss Garnet's Angel,* is about a retired history teacher on an extended visit to Venice. She wanders one day into a side-chapel in St Mark's Basilica where a group of people is being led in silent prayer. Julia Garnet is a 'devout Communist' and unsympathetic to religion but, earlier, she had attended Vespers at the Basilica and had been thrilled by the music.

When she finds herself more or less trapped in the little chapel and sitting in silence, her response is one of discomfort. But she stays. As she overcomes her unease and allows the silence to envelop her, she finds an unexpected peace. She finds more than peace. What Julia Garnet finds in the stillness of that chapel gives us a glimpse of what awaits all who take the way of silent prayer.

'The priest came to the end of the reading and sat down. There was a pause during which Julia Garnet waited for something to happen. After a while it became apparent that nothing was going to happen, except the silence.

'Her first response was annoyance. The vespers in St Mark's had been dramatic. Compared with the threnodic splendour of all that, this abrupt nothingness felt like a cheat.'

But after a while she began to enjoy the silence. Gently, like dripping honey, the quiet filled her pores, comforting as the dreamless sleeps she had fallen prey to.

'The silence was holy. What did "holy" mean? Did it mean the chance to be whole again? But when had one ever been whole? Silently, silently the priest sat in the nameless peace. Julia Garnet sat too, thinking no thoughts.'

Julia Garnet's story is fictional but her encounter with silence describes better than many a long treatise what lies down the road of silence. It reflects what many people feel when they first try to meet God in stillness and silence.

Annoyance, her first feeling, is short-lived. Soon the quiet begins to seep into her being. She begins to reap the reward of staying in the silence. She grasps that the silence is 'holy'. And this realisation leads her deeper into an understanding of what 'holy' means. It means to be whole. The silence and the peace it brings seems to promise a return to wholeness. In welcoming instead of resisting the silence she seems to enter into the 'nameless peace' which surrounds the priest.

As we begin, like Julia Garnet, to leave behind the constant dialogue within ourselves, as we sit like her thinking no thoughts, we too are led into a place of nameless peace, a place of peace where we accept ourselves, where we begin to forgive ourselves, where we begin to become whole again.

44

Becoming Whole Again

In his *Confessions* Augustine describes movingly how God had made him whole after many years of brokenness. 'I find no safe place for myself save in you in whom all my scattered pieces are gathered together,' he writes.

The journey to wholeness, he says, started when he withdrew to the quiet place of sweet solitude within his own heart. There he invited God to speak to him. 'Whisper words of truth in my heart,' he pleaded, 'for you alone speak truth. I will leave outside those who do not believe, letting them stir up the dust in their own eyes, while I withdraw to my secret cell and sing to you hymns of love.

'I shall not turn aside until you gather all that I am into that holy place of peace, rescuing me from the world where I am broken and deformed and giving me new form and new strength.'

Augustine describes that holy place of peace in his commentary on John's Gospel. It is 'that innermost shrine of your deepest self,' he tells us, 'that place of sweet solitude, that secret dwelling where there is no weariness, where no bitter thoughts enter, where there is no lurking temptation or heavy sorrow.'

Looking back on his life Augustine realised that God had been healing him for a long time. All his life, while he had been vainly

115

looking for love in the wrong places, he had been in God's hands.

God's healing touch had rescued him, above all, from self-love. 'You saw me and transformed my ugliness into beauty,' he recalls. 'Like a balm which soothes my pain, your hidden touch healed my self love. And day by day you continued to heal me until the confusion and darkness were cleared from the eye of my soul.'

Augustine sees self-love as the main bar to the love that beckons us towards God. He is aware that unless we are healed within we will be disabled, lacking the confidence and energy and the inner strength to become our true selves.

Our self-love is the result of our lack of belief in ourselves. Too often we accept other people's opinions of who we are. We compare ourselves with others and see ourselves as failures or as inferior to them.

Augustine would have us give up our futile searching for our identity in the eyes of others and go deep into 'the shrine of our deepest selves' to the one who loves us. If we allow the Lord to gather us to himself, to work in us, then the effects on ourselves as well as on others are healing and life-giving. The scattered pieces of our broken self are brought together. Day by day God heals our brokenness and we, too, become whole again.

So Augustine bids us: 'Surrender to him now all your futile searching. What is withered in you will flower again. Your sickness will be healed. What is faded will be fresh again, and what is warped made whole and strong and sound. And all that is weak in you will not drag you to the grave. But your wholeness will abide, will remain with you before God, who remains strong and abides forever' (*Confessions* 4.11).

45

The Lord is at Work

The changes that take place in our times of stillness are often unnoticed by us. Or they seem slight. But they are significant. Even tiny changes in our souls can have long-lasting effects.

One day, on a tour of York Minster with a group from the school where I taught, we stopped before the windows known as The Five Sisters. Our guide invited us to keep looking at the great sea of grey glass. 'Just keep looking,' she said, 'and tell me what you see.'

Our party of schoolboys was silent. Then, one after another, they said: 'I see little red specks.' 'I see green ones.' 'And blue ones.' The longer we stood, the more of these little specks of colour appeared. What at first seemed a mass of grey was soon speckled with colour.

When we first enter the great silence of our hearts, all we may see is a grey landscape where nothing is of interest and nothing is happening. But if we stay and hand ourselves over to the silence, slowly we begin to notice things that, with our restless eyes, we did not at first see. The longer we stay, the more our gaze discovers.

God is always at work in the hearts of those who are searching for him. As we hand ourselves over to silence we are allowing the Lord to work in us. He is moving in the very depths of our being, in the place we call the subconscious. He is at work in those areas where our hurts are buried, where problems and past traumas are deadening our inner lives.

And while nothing seems to be happening on the surface, a lot may be going on in these hidden places. The Lord is at work freeing us, healing us. Only later, often much later, do we become aware that he has visited the darker areas of our being and set us free.

We need a very perceptive eye, like the schoolboys at York, to spot the changes in ourselves at first: a tiny lowering of the level of anxiety perhaps, a feeling of more energy, or an ability to sit with sad memories. Others may notice them before we do. Sometimes a glimmer of the divine light in us shines through.

46

Our Own Hidden Beauty

It is a raw December day, but bright and still. From the top of the Clent Hills the view takes in Warwickshire, Staffordshire, Worcestershire and Shropshire. My moment of delight is interrupted by the faint cry of a sheep. A little way down the side of Calcot Hill I spot a ewe, struggling to escape from a web of briars in which it has become entangled. As I approach, it struggles frantically to get away. But the more it struggles, the tighter becomes the mesh in which it is trapped.

The animal rears in terror as I try to steady it and attempt to pull away the briars that cling tightly to its thick winter wool. When it is free, it races off like a wild thing.

It reminded me of how some people are afraid of God's approach. For some, it takes real courage to sit still before the Lord. It may be difficult at first, particularly if we have a sense of being no good in God's eyes. But be reassured. 'God sees so much more good in us than we see in ourselves,' says Augustine.

And one of the ways in which our lives are transformed by God in our time with him is that we learn to see ourselves through his eyes. To our disbelief, we begin to see our lives through his compassionate gaze. We begin to see the hidden beauty of our inner self.

This is not a result we would expect or, perhaps, believe to be possible. But God is not bound by our expectations.

God's work within us during our time of silence is hidden, hidden from the casual glance but visible to someone who loves us deeply. The transformation goes on in secret. God's healing touch is gentle. Slowly, as our view of ourselves changes, we begin to believe in our own worth. As we grow in compassion towards ourselves our self-confidence blossoms.

We have been so used to seeing ourselves in a critical way that it may be a long while before we start to see the beauty of our inner self, made in the image of God. But when we see it, we cannot hold on to the over-critical image of ourselves that, maybe, has paralysed us. We begin to believe in ourselves.

'In prayer,' Thomas Merton writes, 'we discover what we already have. You start where you are and you deepen what you already have. We have everything, but we don't know it and we don't experience it. All we need is to experience what we already possess. The trouble is, we aren't taking time to do so.'

On our journey into silence, when we do take the time, we become aware of what is truly in the depths of our being. We become aware of the wealth of goodness within. On our journey into silence we begin to recognise ourselves. We are learning to know the person we really are.

47

Totally Transformed

When we want to gauge where we are heading in the spiritual journey, mostly we look at our moral lives. We expect to become better people, and look to see if we are becoming more kind, more patient, less self-indulgent. If we do not see any improvements, we feel we are making no progress through out silent prayer.

But often we look for results in the wrong place. We expect to be morally or spiritually improved. But the results of spending time with the Lord have more to do with love and service to others than interior decoration.

When you are discouraged by your weaknesses, remember that God is trying to draw you to him to give rest for your restless heart. *That* is his first concern. The moral improvements will come from knowing our true selves, from seeing the beauty of our inner selves.

The work of silent prayer is to allow the healing touch of God to transform us at the level from which life itself flows. That is the centre of our being.

Writing about his months of silence in the Sahara desert in *Meditations on the Sand*, Alessandro Pronzato tells us how wrong his expectations were of what he would find. 'For a long time I believed that prayer was a kind of spiritual aesthetics equivalent to psychotherapy or plastic surgery. I had hoped to come out of it with a smattering of contemplation, a sampling of fine sentiments and a dabbing of supernatural grace. I would emerge from the experience, I thought, slightly more humble, obedient, chaste, responsive, generous.

'I have since realised that prayer is never a matter of repairing and retouching. If you allow God freedom of action in prayer, you can expect to be transformed beyond recognition.'

He realised that his prayer had been nothing but an attempt to protect himself from God. 'All I wanted was that God should just be an interior decorator for my artificial spiritual building. I can now see that God has no time for such health and beauty treatment. He does not accept improvement jobs on existing spiritual constructions. Instead he works with the raw materials themselves.'

Pronzato warns us not to expect to see a person scrubbed and perfumed and toned up with celestial vitamins emerging from the experience of prayer. On the contrary, he says, we must be prepared to be totally transformed. 'To accept the dynamism of prayer is to risk becoming unrecognisable. Which is the only way to be recognised by God.'

Augustine suggests: 'Imagine that God wants to fill you up with honey. But if you are already full of vinegar, where will you put the honey? The heart must be emptied and washed out, made clean and scoured, hard work though it may be, so that it be made ready for something else, whatever it may be.'

48

'My Silent Heart Opens Like a Flower"

Elizabeth Rimmer writes about her own wrong expectations in one of her poems:

> I thought perhaps You would come in splendour,
> With choirs of angels and golden majesty;
> And I would sing Your praises through all eternity –
> I have no voice.
>
> I thought perhaps You would come in judgement,
> But You ask no questions, make no accusations,
> Only by your light I see my own sinfulness,
> And Your great mercy.
>
> I thought perhaps You would come in power,
> But You do not ask, or say, or do but only be,
> And in the sun of Your silence, my silent heart
> Opens like a flower.

'My Silent Heart Opens Like a Flower' by Elizabeth Rimmer is reproduced by permission of the poet (www.burnedthumb.co.uk).

PART SIX
THE FRUITS OF SILENCE

49

Living in the Present Moment

One of the first fruits of silence is that we find ourselves able to accept the reality of the present moment. More than that, we feel glad to be at ease in it. As we sit quietly in the Lord's presence our whole attention is focused on just this instant of time.

As we rest in the present moment and our mind becomes quiet, we are freed from the pressures of our past life. They no longer cast their dark shadow over us. In the stillness the heavy clouds pass away and the burden of the past is lightened. The future, we feel, can be left in God's hands. It can be left out there, to be dealt with when the time comes.

Even though we may be dealing with problems, and be deeply troubled when we begin our time of silence, gradually as our mind comes to rest we look at our difficulties in a less anxious way. We see them, but find we are able to look without judging. We are no longer tempted to sort things out, to plan our future action. Just for this present moment we sit in calm acceptance. As our anxious surface self is lulled to sleep we think only of our calm, quiet resting with God and in God.

Being in the present, freed from all the baggage we carry around, is one of the fruits of sitting still, of praying this way. It helps us to be wiser about life, more compassionate, more alert to what needs to be done. Our prayer of silence helps us to see deep into the reality of the present moment and into the life of everything around. We are freed from the muddle in our minds.

To live in the present is to be guided by the Holy Spirit. When we reach that moment we are free, carefree, like the birds of the air, like the lilies of the field. 'Consider the lilies of the field, how they grow,' Jesus told his disciples. 'They toil not, neither do they spin. And yet I say to you, that even Solomon in all his glory was not arrayed like one of these' (Matthew 6:28–29).

Such outcomes are wonderful. Yet we cannot strive for them or make them happen. All we can do is prepare a way for the Lord and leave ourselves in the hands of the Holy Spirit.

50

Filled with Joy

Our prayer of silence is bearing fruit when we feel life as less of a burden and we begin to recover the elusive joy of being in the present moment. Moments when we feel totally present, at home with ourselves. Moments when our thinking ceases for a little, and we *see*.

Wordsworth, in his poem *Lines Written a Few Miles Above Tintern Abbey*, speaks of the serene and blessed mood in which 'the heavy and the weary weight of all this unintelligible world is lightened' and 'we see into the life of things.'

To be at ease in one's mind is to accept with joy the gift of the present moment. It is the ability to see without judging, seeing things as they really are, seeing things as filled with an inner splendour.

To see without judging is to live in delight, to be content to see without straining after meaning or understanding. We are content to let things be. This is true above all of one's own self. We look at ourselves without judging.

In daily life we are so used to seeing ourselves in a harsh, condemning light that we cannot bear to look for long, cannot bear to be alone with ourselves. So, without realising it, we spend our lives running away; anything rather than face who we are, or who we think we are. But when we come to rest in silence and overcome our resistance to being at home with ourselves, we see into our own hearts. We accept ourselves as we are.

The present moment is full of joy if we can allow ourselves to rest in it. We rest in God and we delight in him and delight in what we are doing.

In Yeats' poem *All Souls' Night* an Irish woman, Florence Emery, who was renowned for her beauty and who dreaded the onset of age and wrinkles, took herself off to India as a teacher. There she learned about the soul's journey:

> How it is whirled about
> Wherever the orbit of the moon can reach
> Until it plunge into the sun;
> And there, free and yet fast,
> Being both Chance and Choice,
> Forget its broken toys
> And sink into its own delight at last.

When we come home to ourselves, when we sink into our own delight, we also come home to God, who holds us fast yet leaves us free.

51

A Song in Our Hearts

As we sit quietly in the Lord's presence we begin to savour the sound of silence. All without is silent. All within is silent. There is just God and us. And he is silent too.

In the hushed and sacred silence, words are now mere noise. We stand in God's presence and take a deep breath. Our whole being is gathered together in a reverent hush.

It is as if our whole being is lulled to sleep, drawn into our hearts which stand ready, expectant. We are not expecting God to say anything but we are listening. God is listening.

This is the moment when all is wrapped in silence. Maybe a word comes from deep within, or maybe not. All that matters is openness, attentiveness, alertness. Just being with God and knowing that God is with us. Not trying to understand. Just a calm letting be. The moment is a gift.

Mother Teresa of Calcutta was once asked: 'When you pray, what do you say to God?' She said: 'I don't say anything. I listen.' Then she was asked, 'All right. What does God say to you?' She said: 'God doesn't say anything. God listens.'

And she added: 'If you can't understand that, I can't explain it to you.'

In daily life, when we listen to ourselves, what we usually hear is the jangled noises in our minds. In the silence we pick up another sound. When the mind becomes quiet we pick up the music that is in our hearts. That is an extraordinary discovery.

If we can silence what Augustine calls the din in the mind the inward ear, the ear of the heart, picks up that music which is everywhere, 'if only,' he says, 'the world's noise did not intrude' (*Confessions* 11.10).

Augustine dares to say that if we become totally silent, in body, mind and spirit, we hear a sound that few human ears have ever heard, the sound of heaven's music. Those who know how to be still for long periods hear the music of God's festivity. And this finds an echo in our hearts. They begin to sing.

People who have never heard anything within except the discord of their noisy minds are surprised to find there is a song in their hearts. The touch of God in our lives seems always to stir a song in our hearts and on our lips. It is as if in any encounter with the divine the heart must sing.

The father of John the Baptist broke his long silence with a song, when his son was born. He sang of the 'loving kindness at the heart of our God'. And Mary, mother of Jesus, when she was greeted by Elizabeth as 'the mother of my Lord', broke into song. She sang of the great things the Lord had done for her (Luke 1:46).

When we reach our still centre we, too, find ourselves breaking into song, a song of delight, a song of gratitude, a song of praise. We realise the absolute truth of who we are and this makes the heart sing.

52

The Splendour of Eternity

Augustine tells us very simply that if we can call our mind home and keep our mind still we will get a glimpse of God. 'If only our minds could be held steady they would be still for a while, and for that short moment we would glimpse the splendour of eternity, which is forever still.'

In his *Confessions* he recounts sharing such a glimpse with his mother, Monica, as they rested on their journey back to Africa after his conversion. They were staying with friends in Ostia and it was there a few days later that his mother died.

'Not long before the day on which she was to die,' Augustine recalls, 'my mother and I were alone, by the window which overlooked the garden of the house at Ostia. We talked a long time together and our conversation was full of joy and peace. It seemed as if our hearts were fed from the stream that flows from your fountain.

'We talked about the joys of life and its pleasures and we were sure that no matter how great they were they could not compare with the life of the world beyond death. We seemed to pass beyond all the wonders of your world, even beyond our very selves. And we came to that place of plenty, where you feed us forever with your truth.

'And while we spoke of the eternal wisdom, longing for it and straining for it with all the strength of our hearts, for one fleeting instant we reached out and touched it.

'Suppose, we said, that the noise within were to cease ... Suppose that the heavens and even our own soul were silent, no longer thinking of itself but passing beyond. Suppose that our dreams and our imagination spoke no more. That every tongue and every sign and all that is transient grew silent – for all these things have the same message to tell, if only we can hear it, and their message is this: We did not make ourselves, but he who abides for ever made us.

'Suppose, we said, that after giving us this message and bidding us listen to him who made them, they fell silent and he alone should speak to us, not through them, but in his own voice, so that we should hear him speaking. Suppose that we heard himself, with none of these things between ourselves and him, just as in that brief moment my mother and I had reached out and touched the eternal wisdom that abides over all things. Suppose that were to continue. Would this not be what we understand by the words *Come and share the joy of your Lord*?'

53

A Bottomless Well of Love

Basil Pennington has an image of how stillness allows us to be open to the promptings of God's Holy Spirit. He says: 'I have noticed when a pond is greatly agitated by the breezes or the wind one can throw in a pebble, or even many pebbles, and there is no noticeable effect. When the pond is perfectly at peace and one casts a pebble into it the gentle waves spread in every direction until they reach even the farthest shore.

'I have noticed that in the greater quiet the thoughts, for better or for worse, are much more perceptible. When we are in the midst of a busy life many thoughts go in and out of our minds and our hearts, and we do not perceive the effect they are having upon us. When we come to achieve a deeper inner quiet then we are much more discerning. The way is open to follow even the most gentle leadings of the spirit and to avoid even the most subtle deviations that are suggested either by the self or by the evil one.

'In deep prayer,' Basil Pennington continues, 'with the help of the Holy Spirit, we can hope to so establish this deep inner quiet that even in the midst of everyday activities this lively sensitivity will remain and all activities will be guided by the call of grace and the leading of the Holy Spirit.'

When we enter the deep silence, our prayer is a kind of standing still before God, a kind of gaze of love; being with God without the need to say anything. And at first we have the feeling of losing ourselves in emptiness.

But if we persevere and succeed in keeping still, gradually we will discover that in the silence, in the emptiness, there is a fullness that calms. We discover that the sacred space is full of the activity of God.

In this space, in this sacred leisure, we regain a freshness and nourishment, a feeling of well-being which draws us back with a deep hunger to this quiet prayer, which seems senseless to our active, busy minds, but which fills us with energy, purifying us of the rubbish we collect in our minds.

William Johnson, in his *Letters to Contemplatives,* writes that as the emptiness deepens we carry it around always, 'when one is talking and laughing and teaching and walking and standing on the train. It is there when one goes to sleep at night and when one awakens in the morning.'

This emptiness, what Johnson calls the void, becomes a spring of clear water welling up to life eternal and giving great joy. 'We come to realise the void has a source,' he writes, 'and the source is Jesus, the Word Incarnate, the Inner Guest. And he is opening up the way to an even more immense and limitless and bottomless void which is the Father.'

We are not afraid of this emptiness, Johnson says. It is intensely creative, like 'a bottomless well of love'.

'At first it does not seem like love. You are the log soaked in water; and the fire of love is engaged in burning out the smoke or the dirt. But when this smoke clears away the log catches fire and becomes a living flame of love.'

54

The Divine Spark

'God made our capacity for goodness the innermost part of us,' wrote the fourteenth-century German Dominican, Johann Tauler. 'In this he gave us our greatest likeness to him who is our father, and this wonderful divine spark is deeper inside us and closer to us than we are ourselves.'

The deeper we sink into our silent prayer, the more we become aware of the riches within, of our deepest, original self formed by God in his likeness. We begin to reclaim the gifts which have lain unused, unrecognised within us.

The deeper we go the more we discover. And at the end of our journey inwards we find our wellspring of love, because Love has made its home within us.

The fact is, Thomas Merton writes, that if you descend into the depths of your own spirit, and arrive somewhere near the centre of what you are, 'you are confronted with the inescapable truth that, at the very root of your existence, you are in constant and immediate and inescapable contact with the infinite power of God.'

It comes as a shock to discover this. We have perhaps believed that our basic inclination is towards evil. Instead we discover that our deepest self is in constant union with God. We do not have to struggle to attain this. It is not some extraordinary gift reserved for those who devote their lives to prayer and dedicated love. Rather, it is a fact of our nature, a gift given by God.

Gerard Manley Hopkins, in his poem *God's Grandeur,* writes of 'the dearest freshness deep down things.' In the dearest freshness that lies deep down in us is Love itself, that source of life that Jesus promises when he says, 'Let anyone who believes in me come and drink.' In our deepest self God abides and when we return to this place we find that we are in him and he is in us. This discovery can change the whole direction of our lives.

55

Our Reason for Living

To discover in our silent hours that we are already united with Love itself, that love is the wellspring of our lives, is to rediscover our reason for living. The realisation that our deepest self is in constant union with God begins to colour all we do.

We now discover that there is no need to wear ourselves out trying to please God, to win his love. His love is given. He is a constant in our lives.

Our strenuous efforts to win his love are unnecessary. From now on we can relax and enjoy his love. 'Enjoy being loved at the centre of your being,' says Augustine in his book on the Trinity (*Trinity* 8.7).

We become aware that being in the love is all that matters. In the light of this new awareness we no longer value ourselves because of what we do. Our value is not the sum total of all we *do*. Our value is far greater and independent of that. What we *are* is what matters.

We are in union with the source of life and love. And because our life has at its centre the union with one who is love itself, our deepest reality is our boundless capacity for love.

We do not try to make ourselves acceptable to God or to others by doing good things. Slowly we become aware of our union with Love and begin to live out of that love. So our goal in life changes.

Our goal is to *be* love. How we live now is inspired by knowing that love is our very essence.

'Love God and do what you will,' Augustine tells us. This is often misunderstood. Augustine means that if we truly love God we shall do only what pleases him. 'Love and do what you will,' he says. 'If you hold your peace, of love hold your peace; if you cry out, of love cry out; if you correct, of love correct; if you spare, spare through love; let the root of love be within; from this root nothing can spring but what is good.'

In other words, to live in the love of God, to be aware of God's love within us, is to be freed from self-will and to will only what God wants. All we do will be good if we are centred on the awareness of our union with the God who is Love.

This does not mean that our instincts cease, without a struggle, to drive us to do selfish things. But when we understand that we are love, that we are good and not evil, we will want to live a life of love.

We behave differently when we believe that our deepest instincts are not towards evil. That, deeper still, is our capacity to love. To keep in touch with that deeper instinct is the reason we devote time to silent prayer.

In our faithful attempts to be still we become aware that if we stay in contact with our deepest, truest self, and live our lives in this new awareness which comes to us in the hours of stillness, our lives will be transformed. Being tuned in to what God is doing or saying within, we allow that to be our inspiration and our guide. We act out of what we are hearing from God within us.

56

The Source of Life

To live the new life that is offered us is to draw our energy from the source of life within us. As we have seen, too often we draw our energy from outside.

Now we no longer judge ourselves on our status in other people's eyes, or on our usefulness. We know that we are cherished and loved by God, and our daily prayer of silence keeps us in touch with this source of life and energy.

To draw all our energies together, and to focus them, is the work of silent prayer. 'To make a prayer of our work,' says Augustine, 'we need to spend many hours in prayer, not working.'

'If I can but touch the hem of his cloak,' said the woman in the Gospel story, 'I shall be healed.' She did manage to touch it and she was healed. But Jesus was aware that power had gone out of him and looked to find her. He then praised her faith (Luke 8:43–48).

The power that Jesus radiated was renewed daily in prayer. After a day spent in attending to people he would send his friends away and find a quiet place to pray. Once he stayed 40 days in the desert. St John of the Cross asks what Jesus did for those weeks. And the answer he gives is one word. He did 'nada'. Nothing. Jesus spent the time with the Father in silent communion.

A young doctor, going through a very stressful time in his life, came to our silent prayer group. A few months afterwards he wrote, 'I am pleased to say that my daily double "dose" of meditation is completely changing my life. My energy levels have risen dramatically. I now need two hours' less sleep at night and don't yawn during surgery! Also, slowly, my "cravings" are dropping away.'

In *Souls on Fire* Elie Wiesel quotes an old Jewish rabbi as saying: 'A person who does not keep an hour a day for themselves is not human. To be involved in other people's lives can become too absorbing. In order to give, we must first "be". And our being is rooted in solitude'.

The trouble with most of us is that we try to go on giving even when the energy has been exhausted. We run on empty tanks. It is to fill our empty vessels that we come before the Lord in silence. When we stay a long while in silence, doing nothing, we are allowing the power that is within us to be gathered together and flow through us into the lives of all we meet.

PART SEVEN

OUR RETURN JOURNEY

57

Sharing Our Gifts

When Augustine describes eternity as a time of rest that leads to seeing, he is aware that resting is the key step into our life with God. We rest long. And in our resting a quiet change takes place. Our eyes are opened. As Augustine said, 'We shall rest and we shall see.' But that is only the first half of the journey he urged us to take.

When we reach this point, at which our resting has opened the eyes of our hearts, then we are ready for the journey back. For Augustine continues: 'We shall see and we shall love.' He sees a link between our resting and seeing, and our going out in love. The real test of this kind of praying is whether it leads to loving.

This is not a selfish journey. God's gifts of peace and healing that are poured into our hearts are of course meant to be cherished. But rather than becoming absorbed by the gifts themselves, we ask why these wonderful gifts are given. The answer is: they are not meant to be hugged to ourselves; they are given to us to share.

The gifts we discover within ourselves prepare us for our return journey. They prepare us for our life and work in the world, for our work with God.

Our work with God is a beautiful partnership. It is surely wrong to speak, as many do, of God 'using' us for his work, using us for his own purposes. This kind of language belittles God. And it demeans us.

God respects the dignity of each one of us. He respects our freedom. He does not use people. Rather, he works with us. His wish is to draw us into partnership with him. God invites. We respond. He works alongside us. His love brings out the best in us. His love releases our talents. In all the good things we do in our partnership with him our gifts shine, our personality blossoms.

We are entitled to enjoy and celebrate the great things we are able to do when we are working along with God. We are entitled to sing our own Magnificat.

The messenger whom God sent to Mary was very gracious. The angel began by complimenting her. And when Mary was puzzled about what God was asking of her, the angel was understanding.

So too with us. God comes graciously to us, inviting us to share with him the work of caring for and loving his people. It is surely this gentle, gracious approach of God that draws such a whole-hearted response from many people.

58

Partners

One of my favourite passages in literature comes from Hermann Hesse's *The Glass Bead Game*. It is important to me because it mirrors how I see God working in our lives, our partnership with him. I give the passage in full as it seems so powerful.

Young Joseph Knecht is being put forward for a place in the best school of music in the land. The day comes when he has to present himself to a master who comes to assess him. Pale with fright, he runs to the dormitory. Trembling, he takes his violin and exercise book, and goes to wait in the practice room. A man enters the room …

'A very old man, it seemed to him at first, not very tall, white-haired, with a fine, clear face and penetrating, light-blue eyes. The gaze of those eyes might have been frightening, but they were serenely cheerful as well as penetrating, neither laughing nor smiling, but filled with a calm, quietly radiant cheerfulness. He shook hands with the boy, nodded, and sat down with deliberation on the stool in front of the old practice piano … "Come, let's make a little music together."

'Knecht had already taken out his violin. The old man struck the A, and the boy tuned. Then he looked inquiringly, anxiously, at the Music Master.

'"What would you like to play?" the Master asked.

'The boy could not say a word. He was filled to the brim with awe of the old man. Never had he seen a person like this. Hesitantly, he picked up his exercise book and held it out to the Master.

'"No," the Master said, "I want you to play from memory, and not an exercise but something easy that you know by heart. Perhaps a song you like."

'Knecht was confused, and so enchanted by this face and those eyes that he could not answer. He was deeply ashamed of his confusion, but unable to speak. The Master did not insist. With one finger, he struck the first notes of a melody and looked questioningly at the boy. Joseph nodded and at once played the melody with pleasure. It was one of the old songs which were often sung in school.

'"Once more," the Master said.

'Knecht repeated the melody, and the old man now played a second voice to go with it. Now the old song rang through the small practice room in two parts.

'"Once more." Knecht played, and the Master played the second part, and a third part also. Now the beautiful old song rang through the room in three parts.

'"Once more." And the Master played three voices along with the melody.

'"A lovely song," the Master said softly. "Play it again, in the alto this time."

'The Master gave him the first note, and Knecht played, the Master accompanying with the other three voices. Again and again the Master said, "Once more," and each time he sounded merrier. Knecht played the melody in the tenor, each time accompanied by two or three parts. They played the song many times, and with every repetition the song was involuntarily enriched with embellishments and variations. The bare little room resounded festively in the cheerful light of the forenoon.

'After a while the old man stopped. "Is that enough?" he asked. Knecht shook his head and began again. The Master chimed in gaily with his three voices, and the four parts drew their thin, lucid lines, spoke to one another, mutually supported, crossed, and wove around one another in delightful windings and figurations. The boy and the old man ceased to think of anything else; they surrendered themselves to the lovely, congenial lines and figurations they formed as their parts criss-crossed. Caught in the network their music was creating, they swayed gently along with it, obeying an unseen conductor. Finally, when the melody had come to an end once more, the Master turned his head and asked: "Did you like that, Joseph?"

'Gratefully, with his face glowing, Knecht looked at him. He was radiant, but still speechless.'

God's work with us is like that of the music master with Joseph. He draws the best out of us by accompanying us. We do great things together.

59

Inner Peace

One of the many blessings that flow into the lives of others from our prayer of stillness is that as we become more at peace, this peace can affect others who come into contact with us.

Anthony de Mello writes that we are not much use to others if we are not 'at home' in ourselves for people who come to us for help. 'If you are not at peace with yourself, you will do more harm than good,' he says. That is a sobering thought for everybody who tries to be of use to others.

A Russian saint, Seraphim of Sarov, advises us to seek peace so that others might find God through us. 'Acquire interior peace,' he said, 'and souls in their thousands will find their way to God through you.'

There is a story of a student from Kiev who had heard of Seraphim's holiness and decided to make a pilgrimage to the monastery at Sarov, where Seraphim lived. The young man was deeply troubled, but felt Seraphim could help him. So he set out to walk the 400 kilometres to Sarov.

When he arrived at the monastery, he found that Seraphim no longer lived there. He was directed to a hermitage, an hour's walk away through the Temniki forest in the summer heat. The student found the little hermitage, but there was no sign of the monk. Wandering around behind the little hut he found a tiny figure curled up asleep at the bottom of the vegetable patch. Seraphim had been tending his garden and was taking a nap.

The student was perplexed. He had come a long way to seek counsel from Seraphim, but he felt he dare not intrude on his rest. As he stood there in the presence of the tiny sleeping monk a great peace came over him. The problems that troubled him seemed to be evaporating. The longer he stood, the more at peace he felt. So, without exchanging a word with Seraphim, he turned towards home and found that his inner turmoil had been calmed by this sleeping monk.

Our quest for inner harmony is not something we seek for its own sake. It is a gift to give to share with others. Inner peace is one of the great blessings of life. If we are at peace we will bring peace wherever we go. We create ripples in the lives of all those we meet.

When a peaceful person enters a room, everyone feels more at ease. For those who spend time in stillness, it is a God-filled peace that they radiate. They are not themselves aware of it, but their presence is a breath of God's own peace.

60

A Listening Heart

We may not all acquire the deep peace of Seraphim of Sarov. Such deep interior peace comes from years of being immersed in inner silence. But one thing we can all offer the world is the gift that Solomon chose, a listening heart.

Our prayer of silence is a prayer of listening. But not an impatient listening. And being silent before God prepares us for being silent before others. As we grow in stillness we are able to listen endlessly. We are able to listen in a new way: to listen without judging, to listen without offering advice, to listen in a way that makes others feel accepted. When we listen in this way we allow people to feel free, free especially of the tyranny of self-condemnation. Once people feel they are not being judged they begin to cease judging themselves.

Ministry today is much more about listening than about preaching. Paul Tournier describes priesthood in our time in these words: 'To listen, to understand, to love, to pray.' This is an area of ministry in which we all can share. Listening without judgement and without giving advice makes people feel understood and believed in. And such understanding leads to loving.

Spending time listening in prayer opens the inner ear of the heart. When we listen deeply, we are able to pick up the half-uttered cries for help that reach our ears every day. Most people are too shy to ask directly for our help. Or too proud. They are unable to reveal their woundedness. They may have called out in the past and no one heard them. They may have had their appeals ignored. So they lost faith. They carry their burdens alone. It takes a special ear to pick up the cries of such people.

On a visit to a children's ward I said to the sister in charge, 'It must be dreadful to listen to these little tots cry and not be able to find out what is paining them.' She replied: 'Father, we don't worry so much about the babies who are crying. We worry about the ones who have stopped crying. The ones who cried and cried, and nobody came. They are the ones we are most concerned about, the ones who have given up, but who are crying all the time inside. You can see it in their eyes.'

All around us are people who have stopped crying and need our help. When the surface of our consciousness is calm, we are able to hear not only what people are saying to us, but we hear within ourselves what is troubling them deep within. Our minds need to be emptied and at ease if we want to be able to hear what people are really saying to us.

Psalm 39 reminds us: 'You do not ask for sacrifice and offerings, but an open ear. You do not ask for holocaust and victim. Instead, here am I.'

The sooner we come to our inner stillness and say, 'Here I am, Lord,' the more people God sends us.

61

Our Love-filled Journey

One of the fruits of silence is that it breaks down the barriers that isolate us within ourselves and isolate us from others. Almost imperceptibly, we find that we are open to other people and to the world around us in a way we have never expected. It is as if our becoming aware of our union with God makes us aware of our union with all created things.

In *The Inner Eye of Love,* William Johnson describes ours as a love-filled journey that makes us one with ourselves, one with the human race and one with God. 'This healing of our fragmentedness begins with the call of love at the core of my being, at the centre of my soul. Profound changes take place,' he adds. 'I may seem like a different person to myself and others.'

One way we can tell that we are being transformed is if other people find us more available, more attentive. The more the barriers come down in our time of sitting still before the Lord, the more we can welcome people. Francis of Assisi says, 'It is important for us to draw aside from our busyness, if we are to meet with joy those who come to draw strength from us.'

While we are weary and harassed, we are able to give the people we meet only a small and distracted bit of our attention. In a letter our religious superior wrote to us he said, 'When people come to us priests these days, they often find us so busy and preoccupied that they are loathe to approach us. They get the impression that we have so much on our minds, and so they don't feel able to bother us.'

In our quiet hours with the mystery we call God we recover our freshness and spontaneity. We find we are able to give our whole attention to others. And we begin to know what it is to meet others with joy.

Our attention to others is not much good, of course, unless it is genuine, natural. Too often we encounter 'professional niceness' from other people who may not have the slightest interest in us. Their plastic cheerfulness is shallow and insulting.

Gospel love is the opposite. There is a world of difference between the love that Christ radiates in the Gospels and the artificial smiles and poses that come from our social training.

The hours we spend in silent waiting renew us. Once we have learnt to be open and attentive in our time of stillness, once we have stopped looking at or thinking about self, then we can be open to receive others. More than that, we are able to see them without the distorting lens of our cloudy vision. As Augustine tells us, true seeing leads to loving.

To be able to be with God in silent attention until the din in our minds quietens prepares us for perhaps the greatest gift we have to offer others. We can give them the gift of interested, total, undivided attention. This is surely love at its most unselfish.

62

Standing in Solidarity

A mong the many ways our silent prayer prepares us for helping others is one which is rarely recognised: doing nothing. Doing nothing in our time with God enables us to be with others without wanting to do anything. We are content to be there with them in support. We are 'just there'.

In his *Way of the Heart*, addressed to fellow-ministers, Henri Nouwen writes that compassionate solidarity grows in solitude, in silence and stillness. Compassion is the fruit of solitude and the basis of all ministry, he writes. 'In solitude we realise that nothing human is alien to us, that the roots of all conflict, war, injustice, cruelty, hatred, jealousy, and envy are deeply anchored in our own heart.

'In solitude our heart of stone can be turned into a heart of flesh, a rebellious heart into a contrite heart, and a closed heart into a heart that can open itself to all suffering people in a gesture of solidarity.' And when we stop judging our neighbours, stop evaluating them, we become free to be compassionate.

He advises us not to underestimate how hard it is to be compassionate. 'Compassion is hard because it requires the inner disposition to go with others to the place where they are weak, vulnerable, lonely and broken. But this is not our spontaneous response to suffering.

What we desire most is to do away with suffering by fleeing from it or finding a quick cure for it.

'As busy, active, relevant ministers, we want to earn our bread by making a real contribution. This means first and foremost doing something to show that our presence makes a difference. And so we ignore our greatest gift which is our ability to enter into solidarity with those who suffer.'

Henri Nouwen's message to ministers applies just as much to our own everyday lives, because it is natural for us, too, to want to feel useful, to make a difference. And in our eagerness to help we may be so taken up with our own solutions or plans that we mistake what people really need from us.

But when we truly love, we are content to stand beside others in their struggles and sorrows. When we sit with someone who is in pain or bereaved, broken or confused, without wanting or needing to do, or even say, then we are bringing God's unconditional love and compassion to others.

63

A Heart Full of Love

'We shall see and we shall love, we shall love and we shall praise,' said Augustine. When we reach this stage on our journey, once we truly love, we are well on the road that leads to praise.

Of course, God does not need or want our praise. Still less does he demand it. The need for praise is very human. *We* need praise, and we need to give praise. So how and when do we praise God?

Most or us sing God's praises whenever we pray. There are times when we are comforted and inspired by well-known prayers, times when the words of the Psalms open our eyes to the beauty and immensity of God's creation and to our place in it. We sing the hymns and psalms which others have been inspired to write, feeling the joy of those who wrote them. And our hearts want to join in, giving praise and thanks to God for his works, for his providence.

But there is a world of difference between praise which is a repetition of other people's feelings of joy, and praise that comes from a heart full of love for God. When we catch even the tiniest glimpse of God we are filled with joy. To be aware of his presence, even for a split second, so fills our hearts with love that we must break into praise.

We shall praise God spontaneously when we have caught a glimpse of how lovable he is, how beautiful he is. The poet Patrick Kavanagh must have had such a glimpse when he wrote the line, 'Beautiful, beautiful, beautiful God'.

As we have heard, Augustine believed that the main task in life is to heal the eye of the heart so that God may be seen. When the eye of the heart is healed and opened we see God, and once we see, we instinctively love. We shall love others, and God, and his creation. We shall find the whole world aglow with the presence of God. Once we truly love we shall truly praise. Our whole life, the way we live, will become a song of praise.

As Augustine preaches in one of his sermons: 'Let us praise him not only with voices, but also with our behaviour. Let our tongues praise him, our lives praise him' (*Sermon 254).*

A truly love-filled life is the best praise we can give God.

64

Sing, But Keep on Walking

How do we praise God with our lives? Augustine tells us how. If your heart is longing for God:

> You are praising God when you do your day's work.
> You are praising him when you eat and drink.
> You are praising him when you rest on your bed.
> You are praising him when you are asleep.
> So when are you not praising him?

And in his Commentary on Psalm 144:7 he reminds us: 'If you praise the works of God, then you will also have to praise yourself, for you are a work of God. Here is how you can praise yourself yet not be proud. Praise not yourself but God in you. Offer praise, not because you are this or that kind of person, but because God made you; not because you are capable of doing this or that, but because He works in you and through you.'

Augustine would have us sing our way through life. In one of his sermons he encourages us:

Let us sing God's praises here below.

Let us sing Alleluia to sweeten our toil.

Sing as travellers sing along the road; but keep on walking.

Relieve your toil by singing.

Do not yield to idleness.

Sing, but keep on walking.

What do I mean by 'walking'?

I mean, press on from good to better.

Go forward then in virtue, in true faith and right conduct.

Sing up – and keep on walking.

(*Sermon 256*)

Don't stray off the road, he tells us. Don't go back. Don't stay where you are.

So, make progress in awareness, in searching, in laughter, in loving, in hoping, in the poetry of life.

Sing, and keep on walking. Do not hesitate or turn back. Keep on walking.

Love in order to find God.

ENDPIECE

Let my soul praise you, that it may love you,
that it may proclaim your compassion.
And that it may praise you for your compassion.

The entire universe never ceases to praise you.
It is never silent.

The human spirit turns to you in praise.
Animals, and even lifeless things, praise you
through the lips of those who contemplate them.

So our soul rises from its weariness,
leans on the things you have made,
and through them soars up to you,
who made all these amazing things.
And in you the soul finds strength and is restored.

(*Confessions* 5.2)

SELECTED FURTHER READING

Augustine, *Sermons*; *The City of God*; *Confessions*; *The Trinity*

Bloom, Anthony: *School for Prayer*

Chapman, John: *Spiritual Letters*

Eckhart, Meister: *Sermons*

Eliot, George: *Felix Holt*

Gangaji: *The Diamond in your Pocket*

Hesse, Hermann: *The Glass Bead Game*

Hopkins, Gerard Manley: *Collected Poems*

Johnson, William: *Letters to Contemplatives*

Main, John: *Letters from the Heart*

Murdoch, Iris: *The Good Apprentice*

Merton, Thomas: *Asian Journal*

O'Donoghue, John: *Divine Beauty*

O'Leary, Daniel: *Already Within*

Pennington, Basil: *O Holy Mountain*

Pronzato, Allesandro: *Meditations on the Sand*

Tauler, Johann: *Sermons*

Thomas, R. S.: *Collected Poems 1945 – 1990*

Vickers, Salley: *Miss Garnet's Angel*

Watts, Alan: *Behold the Spirit*

Wiesel, Elie: *Souls on Fire*

Wordsworth, William: *Poems*

Yeats, W. B.: *Poems*